Political Research

What is political research and why is it done?
What are quantitative and qualitative methods?
How do I do research?

Political Research: an introduction has been designed to provide an excellent starting point for those new to the area of research methods. It assumes no prior knowledge of the subject and sets out the key issues involved in conducting research in Politics. It guides students through a complex and often daunting subject by exploring the many concepts associated with the field, as well as offering practical advice on research practices and information resources.

Part I introduces quantitative methods, including: the key issues and concerns; problems of interpreting data sources; using surveys; and analysing official data. Part II introduces qualitative methods, including: using interviews; evaluating existing research; archives; official reports and documents; and focus groups and observational research. Part III offers a practical guide to conducting research at the undergraduate level, including a guide to writing dissertations in Politics, as well as a guide to information resources such as databases, web sites, libraries and archives.

Features and benefits of this textbook:

- briefing boxes and case studies are used in each chapter to illustrate and clarify key concepts, and highlight the practical use of different research methods;
- a useful glossary, giving easy access to definitions of key terms;
- a dedicated web site containing sample material, extra case studies, important links and essential resources for both teachers and students (http://www.routledge.com/textbooks/politicalresearch.html).

Lisa Harrison is Senior Lecturer in Politics at the University of West England.

Political Research

■ An introduction

Lisa Harrison

London and New York

First published 2001
by Routledge
11 New Fetter Lane, London EC4P 4EE

Simultaneously published in the USA and
Canada
by Routledge
29 West 35th Street, New York, NY 10001

*Routledge is an imprint of the Taylor & Francis
Group*

Typeset in Century Old Style by Keystroke,
Jacaranda Lodge, Wolverhampton
Printed and bound in Great Britain by
T.J. International Ltd, Padstow, Cornwall

British Library Cataloguing in Publication Data
A catalogue record for this book is available
from the British Library

*Library of Congress Cataloging in Publication
Data*
Harrison, Lisa.
 Political research : an introduction / Lisa
Harrison.
 p. cm.
 Includes bibliographical references and
index.
 1. Political science—Research.
 2. Political science—Research
Methodology. I. Title.
 JA86 .H35 2001
 320′.07′2—dc21   2001016091

ISBN 0–415–22655–4 (hbk)
ISBN 0–415–22656–2 (pbk)

For Gary

Contents

CONTENTS

CONTENTS

CONTENTS

Briefing boxes

Preface

The remit of higher education in the twenty-first century requires of its students much more than detailed subject knowledge. We are firmly entrenched in a system which demands 'transferable' and 'key' skills. Unsurprisingly, in response to this, we have witnessed a diversification in academic courses which seek to answer not only the questions of 'who', 'where' and 'what', but also the 'how'. Research methods courses, in their various guises, are a central element of any Politics degree. As someone who teaches the subject, I am fully aware of how 'dry' research methods can appear and the challenge has been to write a text which students find informative and engaging.

This book seeks to provide a straightforward yet comprehensive examination of political research methods from the undergraduate perspective. It does not (and indeed cannot) make the research process 'easy', but rather raises the issues and considerations which confront any researchers undertaking their own research – be it quantitative or qualitative. Good research relies as much upon preparation and procedure as it does upon novel ideas, and this text contains many references to existing studies which should help you to comprehend the obstacles faced by those wishing to understand the world of political institutions and actors.

This text could not have been written without the efforts and encouragement of various people. In particular, I am indebted to Wolfgang Deicke and Jane Martin – both made substantive contributions to Chapters 6 and 8 respectively, and helpfully commented on other parts of the text. I should also like to thank Jocelyn Evans of the University of Salford for providing constructive and enthusiastic reviews of the book in its draft form. Needless to say, this text could never have been produced without the support of my colleagues in the Division of Sociology and Politics, University College Northampton, nor without the unflagging patience and perseverance of my husband Gary. Finally, I am grateful to Mark Kavanagh of Routledge, who has demonstrated great patience during the lengthy process of putting what seemed like a 'good idea' into print.

Lisa Harrison
University of the West of England

Chapter 1

Introduction

Political research methods: what does this mean?

In our day-to-day life of watching and reading about political events we are bombarded with a whole range of facts, figures and points of view, and it is usually the case that we will believe, or accept, some information whilst choosing to question other claims. The focus of this text is an analysis of this process of information retrieval and assessment in our role as political researchers – that is, empirical political research. We are not inactive recipients of political information: we make some sort of choice about what newspaper we read, whether to watch the news, which books we read and, indeed, which courses we might study as part of our degree. Obviously, we are not totally 'free' to make these decisions, and most decisions we make are usually subject to some constraints – for example, whether we can afford to buy a newspaper every day; also, during your degree some courses will be compulsory whilst some will be optional.

As members of a social and political system we rarely look at information without applying past experience and knowledge, hence we are always 'judging' what is presented to us. As students of politics you will (hopefully) spend a considerable amount of time reading books, journal articles and newspapers, and will make use of a variety of other source materials (such as surveys and reports) in order to prepare for essays and examinations. Your tutors would also hope that, as your studies progress, you become more aware of, and even critical of, particular debates and arguments. Our experiences in research face similar constraints: what materials are available in our library? is existing survey material easy to obtain? are we able to interview the relevant political actors? The aim of this text is to make 'better' political scientists of you by becoming aware of problems and hurdles which one faces when, first of all, you employ particular information to produce coursework, and second, when you go on to perform hands-on research, such as writing a dissertation.

What does the study of politics involve? Is it political ideas, institutions, attitudes and behaviour, policy making decisions and networks? It is, at different times, all these aspects, and those studying politics as an academic subject will undoubtedly become familiar with all of them at some time. What methods do we use? That will depend upon the subject matter. Indeed, political research is rarely 'ideal', particularly if it involves surveys and interviews, although this does not prevent political researchers from trying to obtain the highest quality of information possible (by adopting what we might call a 'scientific' approach). What this text will do is familiarise you with these different empirical methods (such as comparative analysis and case studies to name but some), suggest when it is appropriate to use particular methods and, most importantly, identify some of the advantages and disadvantages of using different methods. For as Halfpenny (1984, p. 2) suggests: 'Imaginative research is research done with a critical awareness of what alternative ways there are of doing it, of what the advantages and disadvantages of each alternative are, and of why you are doing it the way you are.'

The art of systematic analysis: the development of political science

We can identify within the study of politics a trend away from the term political *studies* in favour of the label political *science*. The first American university chair in political science was established in 1858 at Columbia (Dahl, 1961, p. 764), and since then we have seen a progression and growth of different approaches to political research. What does the term political science, as opposed to political studies, mean exactly? Marsh and Stoker (1995, p. 7) say that: 'by science we mean the organised production of knowledge that demands of its practitioners certain intellectual disciplines, in particular, logical coherence and adequate evidence.'

While the real world of politics and politicians may seem chaotic, as political researchers we cannot afford to ignore the rules of science. This will be elaborated upon in more detail in the next chapter when we examine terminology such as *reliability*, *validity* and *causality*. If we adopt Marsh and Stoker's approach we are claiming that the study of politics involves more than merely accounting for singular findings and events. Rather, we are employing a recognisable process of analysis which includes logic and maybe even prediction.

The term political science is often (although not exclusively) associated with the growth of the behavioural approach. The behavioural approach became a prominent focus of political research in the early part of the twentieth century, and its establishment is associated with the University of Chicago in the United States during the 1920s and 1930s (although the 'Chicago School', as it is commonly known, was heavily influenced by European political scientists). However, the development of the behavioural approach was not just driven by ideas, but also by methodological tools – particularly the availability of surveys for studying political choices and attitudes (Dahl, 1961, p. 765). The label political science is important from a funding level. For example, the Economic and Social Research Council (ESRC) is one of the largest independent funding agencies involved in funding and promoting 'social science research'. Created in 1965, the ESRC has a current annual budget of over £60 million. Without such funding (from the ESRC and many other organisations) we would certainly be severely restricted in the breadth and depth of our political knowledge.

Much of the research we can carry out only begins to have any value when we can use it to support a particular theory. Research data are merely a device we employ to illustrate and reinforce theoretical foundations. Do not be misled into believing that lots of data can be a sufficient substitute for appropriate explanation. Research data should be illustrative, not and end in themselves. We are scientists in as much as we are trying to 'make sense' of a political world which is defined by human thoughts and actions.

In some ways politics is very different to other social science subjects, and in others there is a great deal of similarity. The obvious difference is that we are concerned with political behaviour and institutions, rather than purely historical, sociological or psychological concepts. Yet despite this, these subjects often share the same basic research principles. This is partly because the distinction between the subjects is not always clear cut (one only has to look at a range of book titles – Dowse and Hughes's *Political Sociology*, Childs's *Britain since 1945: A Political History*,

Samuels's *The Political Psyche* – to see that this is the case). Many existing text books focus upon general social science research methods. Indeed, the principles relevant to carrying out an appropriate survey or interview will be broadly similar for any social science. There are some important differences between the subjects though. 'Observation' is a technique common to sociology and anthropology, but it is employed relatively rarely in political research. This is not to say that it cannot be used – it is just not feasible in many cases. For example, we may find it useful to 'observe' Cabinet meetings, but are unlikely to find access easy!

Within political science, we rarely take the psychological approach, which employs experiments to test hypotheses. Any student of psychology will invariably be introduced to the principles of behavioural conditioning in which animals have been trained to respond to particular stimuli (as exemplified by Skinner's rats and Pavlov's dogs). However: 'Social scientists cannot create laboratory conditions and then intervene in the experimental process to see what changes on existing relationships are induced as a result' (Broughton, 1995, p. 26). In the human world, people receive their political cues from a whole range of sources (such as the family, the workplace as well as the media) and it would be unethical for us to control these environments to any great extent. Hence, the main reason for avoiding experimental techniques in political research are similar to the justifications we put forward in relation to observation: it is very difficult to create a totally experimental environment in politics (although not altogether impossible). When might the experimental approach prove to be useful?

In order to assess whether the media can influence voting choices, an experimental study of television news was carried out during the 1997 general election campaign (a more substantial account of this study is provided in Chapter 6). The study tested four hypotheses which were based upon existing theories of media-agenda setting (Norris *et al.*, 1999). Respondents were asked to complete two questionnaires, in between which they were shown a thirty-minute selection of video news, in order to assess whether the news exposure influenced responses. Yet the authors behind this study recognise that while 'experiments provide a more satisfactory way to examine the short-term impact of media messages . . . In contrast, many different factors other than the news media could influence public concerns' (ibid. p. 129). It is simply not possible to create a totally experimental situation in politics, living in the safe hope that, were our scenario to occur in the real political world, our political actors would behave in exactly the same way.

Whilst this text will focus upon the *main methods* used in empirical political research, examples of less conventional methodologies will also be identified and examined. We have stated that a scientific approach to the study of politics is an attempt to produce a 'logically coherent' and empirically supported knowledge, yet in the drive to develop explanations and theories we have to recognise that much of what we research rotates around attitudes, beliefs and interpretations. We can state the turnout in an election with a high degree of certainty, but we are unlikely to be as confident about the precise reasons why some people did not vote. In this sense, the political research method(s) we adopt is often central to our overall findings. It is easy enough to read a book or article and say, 'but the question you really should have asked is . . . ', or 'why did you look at institution *x* and not institution *y* . . . ', or 'it's all right asking people who did vote what they think about New Labour, but what about those who didn't vote . . . '. Any published research worth its salt should have a clear explanation of methods, and I suggest you read this section of any research carefully, and use it as a reference point when reading the rest of the work.

As such, there may be some disagreement as to whether an 'ideal' research method exists. Rather, there are methods which are more appropriate in different circumstances, enabling us to provide more accurate explanations and theories, and this text will predominantly focus upon these. There are several questions we can ask about *all* political research:

Briefing box 1.1 Questions commonly asked of political research

- *Who produced the research?* Was it an academic, a journalist, a politician, a think tank?
- *Why was it produced?* Is it a one-off study or part of an ongoing project?
- *How was it carried out?* What method or methods have been employed? Was the research funded – if so, by whom? What sort of access did the writer gain to the subject studied? How long did it take? How long ago was the research carried out?
- *What is actually being presented?* Are all questions answered? Could other issues have been investigated?
- *What does it mean?* Has it led to policy change? Has it affected political behaviour?

H.
access

Ultimately, the books or journal articles we read, the news bulletins we watch or listen to, and the official documents and archives we search through have been produced for a reason. In some cases there may be a legal requirement or a sense of 'public duty' (see our examination of official data in Chapter 4) whilst other cases may be satisfying a more general 'need to know'. Therefore, it is very important that we give some consideration to who the producers or sponsors are, and for what purpose or circulation it was intended, as their values may (albeit unintentionally) ultimately influence the research process. Hence, the production of research in political science does not take place in a moral vacuum. Research can be as much a result of agenda-setting as it can be deemed to be in the interests of the development of wider public knowledge.

✓ true

The language of political research methods

As with any field of knowledge, political researchers are prone to use technical language to explain their research findings. This is clearly justifiable, as long as those working in the field have a common understanding and interpretation of such terms. However, on the negative side it means that we may be creating exclusive information which is only comprehensible to a small audience.

Problems with terminology are not merely confined to research language. As politics is largely a subjective science, we may also disagree over the meaning of some, very common, political terms. Using clear language in political research is extremely important, as terms such as 'liberal', 'power' and 'development' are notoriously vague and open to multiple interpretations. For example, the term 'government' is a multidimensional concept with at least four interpretations (Finer, 1987, pp. 3–4):

1   the activity or process of exercising control over others;
2   the state of affairs of exercising control, that is, a condition of ordered rule;
3   those in charge in a political system;
4   the style or manner of exercising control, for example, liberal democracy, totalitarianism, military regime.

Therefore, just as we must be clear about the methods we use to research politics, it is vital that we clearly define potentially disputable terms. Throughout this text many technical terms will be identified and explained. Some terms we shall analyse in relation to purely quantitative research (beginning in Chapter 2) and some in relation to qualitative research, whilst some terms are shared between the two. You can also refer to the Glossary for brief explanations of commonly used terms, although by reading the text more fully you will encounter examples of 'real research' which will help you to comprehend the language of political research.

The development of political research methodology: the relationship between political research and theory

How can we be sure that voting behaviour may be linked to economic prosperity or that political interest is related to educational attainment? The political research we carry out helps us to formulate, and if appropriate, revise political theories. Mannheim and Rich (1995, p. 21) claim that: 'theories make facts useful by providing us with a framework for interpreting them and seeing their relationships to one another . . . [they are] sets of logically related symbols that represent what we think happens in the world.'

To reiterate a point made earlier, research data are means to an end. They are of little use if we are unable to relate them to structured, logical explanations. Therefore, theories help us to relate distinct pieces of research to each other. Our research may not always be intrinsically comparative (see below), but we do make use of theoretical foundations in order to assess whether our research findings are unique or whether they fit into a more regular pattern of findings. There are two basic means by which we emphasise the relationship between research and theory. If we take the *deductive approach* we develop our claims, or hypotheses, from existing theory, or to put it in simpler terms, 'we might consider a general picture of social life and then research a particular aspect of it to test the strength of our theories' (May, 1997, p. 30). For example, our theory might state that political party membership is positively related to trade union membership, and when we examine party members we would expect to find that they are also members of a trade union. In contrast, we can take the *inductive approach* in which we build our theory as a result of our empirical findings. For example, we might look at the political affiliations of members of trade unions and then make claims about whether they are members of any (or a particular) political party; or perhaps we can identify a different variable which influences political affiliation, such as membership of particular types of trade unions. In both cases, however, we are relating our findings to an assumption (or theory) of political behaviour – that is, that membership of employment-related organisations and political identification are related.

As you may have noticed, we tend to talk of research methods rather than a singular method. As political science has grown as an academic subject so has the interest in, and attempt to fine tune, the methods of research employed. For example, Blondel's text *Thinking Politically* devotes a single chapter (just seventeen pages) to the issue of methodology. In contrast, the text *Theory and Methods in Political Science* (Marsh and Stoker, 1995) concerns itself solely with the relationship between theory and research, and just as political scientists do not always agree over what it is they study, they also disagree about 'how to do it' (ibid., p. 7). As we shall see in later chapters on survey methods and interview techniques, academics are constantly engaged in assessing the *process* of information collection as much as the actual findings of research itself. We are, therefore, not only seeking the most accurate answers to our political conundrums, but the 'right' methodological approach to achieving this aim. Appropriate research methodology is much more than a mechanical process which can be attained by ticking off a check-list of 'actions to be taken'. Being able to defend our research methodology is as important as being able to defend our findings (in fact, the two go hand in hand). As such: 'By methodology, one does not mean a technique, but an analytical process of defining problems, setting their limits, and finding some means of relating these problems to others already solved' (Blondel, 1976, p. 8). This is something we should bear in mind when reading the research of others too.

Marsh and Stoker (1995) assess the relationship between political research methods and theory in terms of evolving approaches. This began with the normative approach (which is concerned with moral notions of what 'ought to be'), followed by institutional studies (which consider rules, procedures and formal organisations); the behavioural approach (examining political behaviour and attitudes via individual and large-scale studies); rational choice theory (which explores the way in which political decisions are taken); feminism (which attempts to redefine politics from a non-patriarchal perspective); and discourse analysis (where we consider the structuring of social meaning, language and symbols in political debate) (see Marsh and Stoker, 1995, for a greater elaboration of these approaches).

In contrast, Blondel (1976, p. 13) identifies the development of political analysis as a history of the 'three main battlefields', each dominating political analysis at different times. One 'battlefield' has been represented by the distinction between '*normative and descriptive political science*' – that is, the study of what ought to be versus the study of what actually occurs.

Second, Blondel identifies the 'battlefield' between '*law and reality, the problem of structures*', in which a legal approach is taken towards the study of politics. Examples of this approach would be analyses which focus upon constitutional law, public law and administrative law, when 'the problem rotates around the question of implementation of rules, and the role which the notion of rules plays in political life' (ibid., p. 21). The problem here is that political behaviour is influenced by a range of structures and procedures (for example, the family or membership of a political party) which lie beyond the remit of legal rules.

Blondel's third 'battlefield' is that between *the unique and the general*', in which we have witnessed a move towards the quantification of political analysis and the development of 'behaviourism' (which first developed in the USA). It is this approach which marks the difference between political *studies* and political *science*.

Hence, what is clear is that we can take different approaches to the study of political life; and a strong relationship exists between the theoretical beliefs and underpinnings that prompt our research and the methods which we find most 'appropriate'. Rather than consider the historically developed approaches to political research, this text focuses upon 'types' of empirical research methods. The main distinction made here is between the use of quantitative and qualitative forms of data and the analytical frameworks in which such information is employed. So, for example, we shall consider research which is operationalised via case studies and research which is operationalised via comparative analysis. How do these two research designs differ? Rose (1991, p. 446) claims that comparison is 'one of the oldest forms of the study of politics, tracing its roots back to Aristotle', which can be defined by its 'focus and method'. For Rose (ibid., p. 447), comparative analysis includes the following criteria:

- it includes more than one country: a study of only one country is a case study;
- it uses concepts which are applicable in more than one country – the concept 'general election', for example;
- it rejects universalism and particularism in favour of 'bounded variability'. That is to say, political systems will always be different to some extent, but there are limitations, or 'boundaries', to these differences. For example, we tend to define political legislatures as unicameral (consisting of a single legislative house – as is the case in Denmark, Finland and Portugal) or bicameral (parliaments with two chambers – such as in Austria, France and Spain). The classification of legislatures is limited rather than infinite.

Comparative studies begin with what Rose terms a 'matrix' – rather like a table in which we can 'tick off' characteristics as they appear. The beginning of comparative analysis involves two decisions: which countries and which concepts, and 'the more countries examined, the fewer the concepts; the fewer the countries, the more detail, approaching holistic comparison' (Rose, 1991, p. 453). Yet it may be difficult to identify *true* comparative analysis as 'even the most insular types of works frequently contain references to other countries' (Page, 1990, p. 438).

'The Comparative Method' is explored in some detail by Mackie and Marsh (1995). Its major strength is that it avoids 'ethnocentrism' (ethnocentrism occurs when we are insensitive towards the social context of what we are researching, or when we are unaware of historical and cultural differences – that is, we view what we are studying from our own personal and cultural perspective). However, it would probably be more appropriate to refer to comparative *methods* rather than to a singular method. This is because comparative analysis can take different forms. It can be used to retest earlier studies – a comparison of individual case studies over a period of time. It can also be used to compare across types – for example, parliamentary procedures in different countries, voting behaviour in different regions, economic development across continents.

The development of comparative analysis has grown rapidly since the 1960s, aided by the popularity of quantitative analysis and the development of data archives, although such research tends to focus upon the industrialised nations (and more recently upon the newly democratised nations of Eastern Europe), and upon studies in the field of international relations (particularly as globalisation has been marked by a rise in the numbers and importance of supranational political organisations). Its popularity and importance as a research approach is highlighted by the fact that the European Consortium of Political Research has been established to promote the comparative study of politics.

Conclusion: the necessity of a scientific approach towards political research

Within this chapter we have highlighted the central relationship that exists between understanding the political world and appreciating how we arrive at this understanding. As Shively (1998, p. 2) claims: 'Social research is an attempt by social scientists to develop and sharpen theories that give us a handle on the universe. Reality, unrefined by theory is too chaotic for us to absorb.'

Certainly, the world of politics may often appear chaotic, and also secretive and exclusive. By appreciating the strengths and weaknesses of various political research methods we are able to justify our theories, understandings and explanations. What this text now seeks to do is identify a range of empirical methods and studies within political science which will enable you to understand how we might carry out research projects, and more importantly the advantages and disadvantages we might face by employing such methods.

Part I will introduce the topic of quantitative research. Chapter 2 focuses upon the terminology involved and some of the general strengths and weaknesses of the quantitative approach, and includes two case studies to illustrate how quantitative data is employed in political research. Chapters 3 and 4 look at particular aspects of using quantitative research. Chapter 3 focuses upon the development and employment of surveys in political research and illustrates the strengths and weaknesses of surveys by scrutinising the role of opinion polling. Chapter 4 examines the use of official data, and in particular the political nature of official statistics.

In Part II we consider the use of qualitative methods in political research. Chapter 5 provides a general overview of the advantages and limitations of such an approach in political research. Chapter 6 offers a practical guide to using interviews as a method of gaining political information.

In Part III, Chapters 7 and 8 focus upon how we can employ existing information in our research, through employing sources such as the media, official documents and personal accounts.

The final section of this text provides some practical hints and suggestions for those about to embark on their own research project (usually referred to as a dissertation). This is not a simple, all-embracing account of what a dissertation should be like, but it does cover some of the most common mistakes which dissertation students regularly make, and which (with sufficient preparation) can easily be avoided. The final chapter of this book provides a reference section of useful information sources which are commonly used by political scientists.

Further reading

There is a plethora of social science research texts which vary in both their accessibility and appropriateness for undergraduate politics students. J. Blondel's *Thinking Politically*, Harmondsworth, Middx: Penguin, 1976, is a useful text to start you thinking about what the study of political science entails and how the academic study of political science institutions and behaviour has developed historically.

D. Marsh and G. Stoker (eds), *Theory and Methods in Political Science*, London: Macmillan, 1995, provides a thorough account of the different theoretical approaches to political research which were briefly mentioned in this chapter, and also includes an introduction to the methodological issues which will be dealt with in greater detail in this text.

The journal *Political Studies* (volume 39 no. 3, September 1991) includes a number of articles which consider the issue of methods in political science (covering topics such as comparative analysis, international relations, the relationship between the study of history and the study of politics, the rational choice and feminist approaches to political analysis, and the theory and methods employed in the study of public administration).

Part I

QUANTITATIVE RESEARCH

Chapter 2

Introducing quantitative analysis

Why do we need to quantify politics? What does the quantification of politics involve?

To reiterate the focus of the discussion in Chapter 1, as political researchers we are looking for patterns and regularities in attitudes and behaviour in order to provide explanations, which we couch in terms of 'theories' (Rose and Sullivan, 1993, p. 9). What we are often interested in understanding is not a physical entity – that is, we cannot 'touch' party preference or political attitudes. Therefore, in order to be able to make any valuable assessment of political characteristics, we have to make use of 'concepts'. If we want to say a country is more democratic than its neighbour, or that one electoral system is more proportional than other systems, we need to be able to put our findings into a quantifiable form. As such, quantitative political research refers to the use of measurement in the analysis of behaviour and attitudes. Its development is associated with the positivist school of research, established in the nineteenth century, which represented a desire to create a 'science of society' and which attempted to mirror the respectability of the sciences of the physical world (Reid, 1987).

The impetus for statistical analysis in the Victorian age derived from the desire of scientists to understand, and thus control, the social world in which they lived. For many people, the term 'scientific' holds notions of legitimacy and authority. Hence, figures such as Marx and Engels employed statistics to develop 'the laws of society'. By the 1840s, statistical societies existed in both Britain and America, although research using social statistics was largely concentrated in America until well into the twentieth century. In this chapter we shall: explore why any quantitative analysis you carry out should be rigorous; begin to introduce some of the terminology that political researchers often use; introduce different types of statistical analysis which may be used in political science; and conclude with two case studies – the first introducing the SPSS program, and the second introducing the contribution of the British Election Studies to political analysis.

In order to carry out appropriate quantitative analysis we need to be precise and rigorous throughout the research process. Being systematic and clear when we employ statistics, Reid (1987, pp. 11–13) suggests, is important for three reasons:

Measurement

We must be clear about what we are measuring. Remember we raised this issue in Chapter 1 when we discussed the notion of multidimensional concepts that are often used in political analysis, for example, 'government'. As political researchers we are often interested in measuring concepts which are unobservable. For instance, when carrying out a survey we may be able to make an accurate guess at whether someone is male or female, but can we make quite so accurate a guess as to whether someone is working class or middle class? Probably not. All social sciences rely heavily upon fluid concepts. Therefore, it is imperative that we use clear definitions of concepts such as 'voter preference' and 'unemployed'. For example, we might choose to define 'voter preference' as the political party that a person always votes for. However, we might quickly find that some people do not always vote for the same party, and this could be for several reasons:

- the voter may have once voted for a particular party all the time, but has recently decided to vote for a different party;
- the voter would like to vote for a certain party all the time, but that party does not always put up a candidate for election, forcing the voter to vote for a second-preference party;
- the voter always votes for the same party in a general election, but chooses a different party for other elections (for example, European Parliamentary elections, local elections) as issues vary in importance.

Therefore, we might have to refine our original definition and state that a voter has a clear voter preference *only if* they have voted for the same party on the last three occasions at which they registered a vote. Similarly, when we come to define 'unemployed' do we mean those who are officially registered as unemployed, or all those who are not in full-time employment (housewives, students and the retired)? (We shall consider the extent to which different people can define social class in different ways in the section of this chapter entitled 'Validity and reliability'). Thus, many of the concepts we employ in political research require careful clarification. It is not necessarily a problem if we are able to use different measures for the same phenomenon, but it is important that we are clear in defining the measures we are using.

Comparison

In Chapter 1 we briefly defined what we mean by comparative studies, and emphasised that this research approach has become increasingly popular since the 1960s. If we are carrying out quantitative research, we put concepts into numerical and statistical form (such as percentages) to enable comparison. Statistics are probably the easiest and most effective way of supporting an argument. If we are analysing research that includes thousands and even millions of people, it is much easier to use percentages to put forward our point. For example, it is easier to understand if we say that 16.8 per cent of voters supported the Liberal Democrat Party in 1997, than if were to say 5,242,947 voters.

The use of comparison in political research is demonstrated by the text *Passages to Power* (Norris, 1997a), which employs a 'common analytical framework' and survey data from nineteen advanced democracies in order to provide a comparative account of legislative recruitment. In order to operationalise (carry out) the comparison, the concept of 'legislative recruitment' is defined as consisting of four components, which are outlined in Briefing box 2.1. It is vital that each country is analysed using the same criteria before comparisons can be made, and thus any arguments that legislative recruitment is similar or different can be validated.

Control of uncertainty

We need to be able to recognise which changes and differences in our research are important and which are relatively trivial. One of the common mistakes that social

> **Briefing box 2.1 Norris's four components of legislative recruitment**
>
> - The structure of opportunities set by the political system;
> - the formal process of candidate recruitment within parties;
> - the demands of a party;
> - the supply of candidates.
>
> Source: Norris (1997a, p. 11)

scientists make is the suggestion that a change or difference is 'significant'. How can we tell exactly whether a difference is of minor importance or of much greater importance?

A useful example of defining significance can be illustrated by the case of the 1997 General Election. This was certainly an important election for several reasons: it marked the end of a long period of Conservative government (18 years); the Labour Party won an overwhelming majority of the seats (63 per cent); and more female MPs were elected than had previously been the norm (18 per cent). These changes were undeniable, but what really interests psephologists (those who study elections and voting behaviour) is why this happened. Did 1997 mark a 'significant' change in voter allegiance or was it merely an attempt by a disgruntled electorate to get rid of a government in disarray? Hence, the text *Critical Elections* (Evans and Norris, 1999) provides an analysis of various aspects of the election (such as party manifestos, social alignments and issue alignments) to see 'whether, in what respects and by how much, the 1997 election differs from its predecessors' (p. xix). That is to say, what the authors really want to know is whether a real shift occurred in voting behaviour or whether voters will return to more traditional voting patterns in the future.

Significant changes/differences can be identified through statistical tests, as we shall show in this chapter. However, the way in which we present statistics is crucial as it can affect the strength of persuasion and it may influence whether others are prepared to accept what we are saying. What we *cannot* do with statistics in political science is prove anything as there is no such thing as final, incontrovertible proof. Hence, we should think in terms of probability rather than certainty.

Obviously, there is a vast wealth of numerical data already available in the world, ranging from economic performance indicators, to official statistics, to candidate electoral performance; and much more is being produced on a daily basis. What we need to decide is what data to use. An initial distinction we can make is between primary and secondary data: 'Analysing data that were collected for some other reason or by some other organization is called *secondary analysis*, as contrasted with the *primary analysis* which you carry out on data you collect yourself' (Fielding and Gilbert, 2000, p. 4). Secondary data is information created by someone else. So we are employing secondary data whenever we quote statistics from books, articles or newspapers, or when we make reference to poll and census data, or to the EU *Eurobarometer* poll (Miller, 1995, p. 155). Obviously, the sources of secondary data are widespread and it would be impossible to list them all here. It may be that you need to collect primary data for your dissertation, and the practicalities of this will be analysed in later chapters.

The language of quantitative analysis

Types of data

Students can often feel disconcerted by the language of statistical analysis. However, much of the technical language that is employed does in fact have a relatively simple explanation and should not be feared. This section will introduce you to some of the most frequently encountered terms and illustrate their role in our understanding of quantitative political research. Statistical data may be at different levels, and the level of data influences how detailed, or 'informative', the information is. Data can be presented on one of three levels.

Nominal

This is the most basic level of data, and the information is coded in terms of discrete categories (often mutually exclusive): for example, gender, party membership (we do not usually expect people to be members of more than one political party at any one time), voters and non-voters at a particular election. Also, we often put large quantities of data into smaller categories to make it manageable. For example, in a large-scale survey we make ask every respondent his/her age, but for purposes of analysis we group together a range of ages (see Briefing box 2.2).

It is clear that in relation to these two categories (gender and age), participants in the survey can only fit into one category for each variable (characteristic). In relation to age, one cannot fit into the group 26–35 and the group 46–55 simultaneously!

Briefing box 2.2 An example of nominal categories

Political participation survey

Total number of respondents = 200

Male = 125   Female = 75

Age: 18–25 = 12   26–35 = 82   36–45 = 75   46–55 = 24   55+ = 7

Ordinal

This is the next level of data, and is also referred to as ranked data. It accounts for data which we can place in some sort of comparative order (which we cannot do with nominal data), for example the results of a leadership contest (see Briefing box 2.3).

We can tell from this that Kenneth Clarke received more votes than his rivals, but this has only limited use as we do not know how many more votes – was it a close contest between all three candidates? We do not know. The same principle applies to placing individuals on a political scale. We can use information about political party

---

Briefing box 2.3 An example of ordinal political data

Results of the second round of the Conservative Party leadership election, 17 June 1997:

Kenneth Clarke   1st
William Hague   2nd
John Redwood   3rd

Source: 'Chronology of Events 1997' in Denver *et al.* (1998, p. 233)

---

supporters to place voters on a scale which ranges from left wing to right wing (see Briefing box 2.4).

We can use information about attitudes towards public spending, support of trade unionism and support for party leaders to place respondents on this scale. The problem is, we do not know if the places on our line are equally dispersed – it may be that the centre party (the Liberal Democrats) is in fact closer to the one on the left or right of the line than it is to the other. Similarly, we can say that someone is *more* right wing, but would it make sense to say they are *twice as much* right wing?

Briefing box 2.4 An example of a left–right political scale

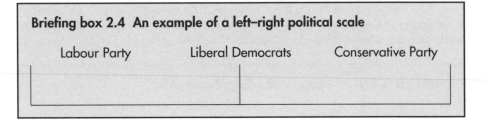

Labour Party   Liberal Democrats   Conservative Party

Interval/ratio

This is often described as the most 'useful' level of data because it also indicates some level of distance. The basic difference between the two is that ratio data has a meaningful zero point whereas interval data does not:

> *Interval data* may be used to calculate how far apart measures are: there are equal intervals or equal distances between each of the measures on the scale. However, with interval data there is no *absolute zero* point. Thus it is not possible to divide or to multiply one score by another . . . Someone who scored 80 per cent in an exam will not necessarily be twice as good or know twice as much as someone who achieved a score of 40 per cent.
>
> (Calder, 1996, p. 227)

Age, for example, is ratio data. From the moment people are born they gain age – first hours and months, then years, and we would not say that someone has a minus age.

Income can also be classed as ratio data as someone cannot earn less than nothing. In contrast, we can refer to temperature as having a minus value, and this is still meaningful. It is unusual in political science that we use interval data (Fielding and Gilbert, 2000, p. 15).

If we go back to the example of the Conservative leadership election, we can tell who came first, second and third just by looking at the votes polled, but we can also tell that the difference between support for Kenneth Clarke and William Hague was very close (only two votes), whilst Kenneth Clarke received more than 1½ times as many votes as John Redwood. The data in Briefing box 2.5 are, therefore, much 'richer' than the data in Briefing box 2.3.

Briefing box 2.5 An example of ratio political data

Results of the second round of the Conservative Party leadership election, 17 June 1997:

Kenneth Clarke	64 votes	1st
William Hague	62 votes	2nd
John Redwood	38 votes	3rd

Analytical terms

We employ particular terminology to not only describe our data, but also to explain the way in which it is analysed. I shall begin in the next section with a few terms which frequently appear in political research but which can often be misinterpreted by an untrained mind.

Populations and samples

As the group of subjects we wish to study increases, it becomes increasingly difficult to study every single example (in fact a study of the whole population would be referred to as a *census*). For example, it would, in principle at least, be much easier to survey all Labour Party MPs than it would be to survey all Labour Party members. Therefore, much of our research relies upon making assumptions about the population based upon findings made at the sample level. What is a population? It is a group which shares characteristics to which we apply an explanation, for example, civil servants, party members, the unemployed.

The first challenge you may encounter as a researcher is identifying the full remit of your population – or what is referred to as the 'sampling frame'. For example, imagine you wished to research former female prospective parliamentary candidates to evaluate their experiences of the selection process. How exactly are you going to locate accurate (that is, complete) lists? The main problem a researcher faces is that sampling frames can quickly become outdated and, as a result, potentially unrepresentative. Think of the electoral register: although it is regularly updated it becomes less accurate as people move house or die. If the sampling frame is unrepresentative, it is likely that any sample chosen from it will also be unrepresentative of the research population. Therefore, accessing records and lists is one challenge, but 'locating the elements of a population' can be a much broader problem (Schofield, 1996, p. 28).

Once we have successfully located a sampling frame we then need to establish sampling units; that is, the characteristics which enable us to break down the population into smaller groups (such as age bands or geographic location). Perhaps the most difficult task facing researchers is selecting the sample so that we can accurately make assumptions about the population. Sampling units should not overlap and should exhaust the entire research population (ibid., p. 27). There are two main approaches: probabilistic and non-probabilistic sampling.

Probabilistic sampling

Briefing box 2.6 Examples of probabilistic sampling

- Random sampling;
- systematic sampling;
- stratified sampling;
- cluster sampling.

Random sampling

This implies that every member of the population has an equal and independent chance of being selected. Indeed, 'random sampling is similar to tossing a coin, throwing a dice or drawing names from a hat' (Schofield, 1996, p. 31). This is not as easy as it sounds, and it is increasingly problematic when the population is large. For example, telephone sampling is becoming an increasingly popular method for assessing public opinion, but it can be criticised because not everyone has a phone and not everyone is listed in the phone book. It is a common misconception that surveys carried out on busy streets are random. Just because the people who are surveyed have not been pre-selected, this does not make them a random sample. People walking down any particular street at any particular time are not truly 'typical of the population' because the types of people we would expect to meet vary. This could, for example, be influenced by the time of day (many people are working mid-morning and mid-afternoon, older people are less likely to be out very late at night), the region or the neighbourhood in which the survey is carried out, or a range of other factors. Computer programs are available which can randomly generate numbers.

Systematic sampling

This is the selection of every *n*th case. For example, by sampling every thirtieth name on the electoral register we are unlikely to get two people from the same household, or even their neighbours.

Stratified sampling

This method entails the division of the research population into sampling units, then applying random sampling to each unit. For example, if we wished to measure the political preference of a student body we might split students into age groups and then take a random sample from each age group.

Cluster sampling

This can be useful if we do not have a sampling frame. If, for example, we are unable to access an electoral register we might choose to carry out a survey among constituents as they visit their MP's surgery. This would be a 'cluster' of the local electorate. Schofield (1996, p. 35) points out that this approach may be the only method which we can employ to survey particular groups, such as the unemployed and homeless.

Non-probabilistic sampling

Non-probabilistic (or non-random) sampling occurs when we hand-pick samples for characteristics or properties. For example, we might want to study only those aged 18–25, only women, only people who read tabloid newspapers. Non-random sampling can take a variety of forms (see Briefing box 2.7).

Briefing box 2.7 Examples of non-probabilistic sampling

- Quota sampling;
- convenience sampling;
- volunteer sampling;
- snowball sampling;
- purposive sampling.

Quota sampling

We identify a number of respondents from particular social strata (sampling units) which proportionately reflect the number of cases in that unit. This method is widely used in market research. For example, if we wish to study people who belong to a pressure group, and we believe that a certain percentage of that particular group's members are female, we should ensure that the same percentage of our study sample is female. There is a potential problem in that the researcher may not identify all relevant and contributing variables and characteristics, or indeed that, as we try to deal with one source of bias, another source is introduced (Schofield, 1996, p. 36). For example, attitudinal differences between pressure group members might be more strongly influenced by age than by gender. Furthermore, it may be easy to identify some sampling units but not others. In relation to pressure group members, we may be able to identify units such as gender and age but not the ones for educational attainment or occupation.

Convenience sampling

As the phrase describes, we pick samples which are easily accessible (such as friends, relations or students at your university).

Volunteer sampling

This takes the forms of phone-ins on TV and radio and postal questionnaires. These are not likely to be truly representative samples, as participants might be personally motivated to become involved. For example, they may hold particularly strong views on an issue. However, this does not mean that we cannot use this method. Wring *et al.* (1999) employed a postal questionnaire in order to examine political engagement among young people, although they 'recognized the possibility that only the more "political" young people in our study might respond' (p. 207) and as an attempt to overcome this problem offered all the respondents the chance to win music vouchers.

Snowball sampling

There are occasions when we really do not have access to a list of all the people who belong to the group we wish to study. Snowball sampling is a sampling technique employed when we might ask a small sub-group to identify others whom we could also study; for example, the members of an extremist or underground group. The problem is that we rarely know the true population size and therefore it is difficult to defend representativeness. This method was employed by Devine in order to analyse working-class evaluations of the Labour Party. This study was conducted via interviews with shop-floor workers, and 'interviewees were introduced with the help of contacts in the town' (Devine, 1992, p. 163).

Purposive sampling

The sample is hand-picked because the participants are typical or interesting examples of what we are researching. This is more likely to be employed in qualitative research than quantitative research.

So what sampling method is 'best'? Ultimately, no sample is ideal and the approach we take will probably be a balance between the amount of precision we require, what we know about the population and the resources which are available. As such: 'representative samples are almost always impossible to obtain. This is because the sample needs to be representative not just on one, but on *every* characteristic that could be relevant' (Fielding and Gilbert, 2000, p. 228).

We shall examine the issue of sampling in more detail in Chapter 3, when we look at surveys.

Inferences

We make inferences when we use a small sample to make judgements about the larger population (as is the case with opinion polls, which we shall examine in more detail in Chapter 3). We tend to make inferential judgements in quantitative research, although this does not exclude their being used in qualitative research. Inferences are a valid research tool if we use a *truly* representative sample, but problems arise if we overlook certain relevant groups, for example, if we only include people who have already decided how they will vote when we study party popularity. Inferences can become problematic whenever we do not accurately represent groups in relation to gender, race or class divisions. We employ statistical formulae to make inferences.

Causality

Within quantitative political research we often discuss our analysis in terms of variables which may, or may not, influence political outcomes. The ability of a characteristic (or variable) to affect attitudes or behaviour is referred to as causality (see Briefing box 2.8).

Briefing box 2.8 Examples of possible causal relationships

Independent variable change	→	Dependent variable change
Age	→	Voting behaviour
Occupation	→	Party membership
Income	→	Political activity

If we are able to ascertain that a causal relationship exists between an independent and a dependent variable, we would expect change in the independent variable to result in a change in the dependent variable.

Significance

Beware of throwing around crucial terms such as significance. Just because we find more people prefer party leader x to party leader y does not mean we have a 'significant' finding. This may be a unique result (what we might term a fluke), or it may be indicative of a normal trend. The term significance can take on two interpretations:

> In statistical parlance, it refers to the likelihood that a result derived from a sample could have been found by chance. The more significant a result, the more likely that it represents something genuine. In more general terms, significance has to do with how important a particular finding is judged to be.
>
> (Blaxter *et al.*, 1996, p. 200)

When we use statistical tests (see below) we employ 'levels of significance' to test the confidence or certainty of these findings, although we can never be absolutely certain that our findings are correct.

Correlations

A correlation measures the extent to which the changes which occur in two variables or attributes are related to one another. These are also known as measures of association. For example, we may wish to test whether a correlation exists between age and voting intention. Briefing box 2.9 outlines the ways in which we identify variable relationships.

Briefing box 2.9 Examples of correlational relationships

A positive correlation The changes in the two variables go in the same direction. For example, we might find that voters are more likely to vote for a 'Party X' as they get older. As a person's age increases, so does their propensity to vote for Party X.

No correlation The two variables are unrelated; for example, the number of cups of coffee drunk per day and level of interest in politics. We would not expect people to be interested in politics purely because they consume a certain amount of coffee.

A negative correlation As one variable increases, a relative decline occurs in the other variable. For example, the more strongly we favour European integration, the less likely we are to vote for an anti-EU party.

A correlation measure will lie between +1 (a perfect positive correlation) and −1 (a perfect negative correlation). Although this is mathematically possible, in the social sciences we are unlikely to reach a perfect correlation of either type.

Correlational relationships provide an ongoing puzzle faced by those who wish to explain the influence of political communications. It has regularly been demonstrated that those who pay most attention to political news are more politically knowledgeable than those who pay little or no attention. But this is like the chicken and egg scenario: do these people know more because they pay more attention, or does their existing knowledge drive them to seek further information?

Beware! Evidence of a correlation does not necessarily mean that we can also imply causality. We might find that 90 per cent of left-handed people vote Labour, but this strong correlation does not mean that left-handedness decides voting behaviour – it lacks theoretical credibility. Therefore, you should not go mad testing for correlations. Such a finding is not likely to revolutionise traditional thinking about voting behaviour. We might find that a whole range of variables demonstrate similar patterns of change, but if we claim this is a valid association when in fact it is not, we are making a 'spurious association' (Bernstein and Dyer, 1992, p. 13). Parsimony can be a valuable trait.

Validity and reliability

One of the main problems faced in trying to develop enlightening research is that accusations are often made that the interpretation of data is *unreliable* or *invalid*. We have stated earlier that in order to have a common understanding and agreement about any political discourse, we need a common dialogue about what social measurements should mean. A classic example is *social class*. What does this term mean? Do we all assess social class in the same way? No. In fact, in order to determine social class we draw upon a range of measures.

We may use *objective social status*. This means we use a range of indicators such as education, income and occupation to decide which social class somebody falls into. All our indicators may point to the same social class, but equally they may all differ. For example, to what class does someone belong if they are public school educated but unemployed? Similarly, to what class does someone belong who is a semi-literate business entrepreneur worth millions?

Alternatively, we may use *subjective social status*. This means that we allow people to self-judge themselves to determine which class they belong to. The problem is that people's definitions of social class may be very different to our own and everyone else's, and indeed they may be subject to feelings of social desirability (might people tell slight untruths about their social class to a total stranger carrying out a survey?). Therefore, in political science an imperfect relationship exists between the definition of social concepts and the accuracy of measuring them, a problem which is constantly being addressed by ongoing research.

If something is reliable we hold certain expectations of it, notably that the findings represent a degree of consistency (Black, 1993). What this means is that, if our research findings are reliable, we would expect to get the same results time and time again. A measure is valid if it actually measures what it claims to measure; for example, a relationship really does exist between the concept and the measure. Therefore, we may end up with a measure which is reliable but not valid, but something *cannot* be valid but unreliable – validity implies reliability and other things as well.

Remember our earlier example in which we claimed that we might find that 90 per cent of left-handed people voted for the Labour Party in the last election. Indeed, if we test over time we might consistently find that left-handed people vote for the Labour Party. Yet as a theory of voting behaviour this is not valid – there is no relationship between the concept of voting behaviour and what we have measured.

The accuracy of our data can be affected by different *types* of unreliability. Black (1993, pp. 78–79) identifies three research approaches which may help us to attain reliable research:

1   *Stability*   By employing a test–retest method we can measure the long-term predictability of our research. This may be useful for ascertaining 'factual' types of information, for example, we may ask someone at six-monthly intervals whether they voted in the last General Election. If their recollection wavers at any time, we may have reason to question the reliability of their other responses too. However, we would not necessarily expect all political attitudes and beliefs to remain the same, particularly over a long period of time (we would live in a very dull political world if they did!). Therefore, just because some responses change they are not necessarily unreliable.

2   *Internal consistency*   We use a homogeneous (similar) set of questions in order to establish the consistency of attitudes. This might be necessary if we were concerned that what we are getting is an artificial response. We are often involved in asking people to rate the importance of certain policies to which they may not pay a great deal of attention in their everyday lives. If someone replies that 'spending on education' is a fairly important issue, do we know whether this is a genuine response, or one that is just picked for convenience? It may be more useful, when constructing a survey, to include several question based around the same topic. If the respondent gives the same response each time, we might assume that it is a consistently reliable opinion, but if the respondent gives a different reply each time then we might begin to question the reliability of their response. Indeed, research has shown that the particular placing of items on a questionnaire could influence the reply that respondents give (Heath and Pierce, 1992; Bartle, 1999).

3   *Inter-judge reliability*   This may be useful when we attempt to assign a large range of occupation descriptions to a smaller number of class categories, and is also important if we need to classify responses to open-ended questions into quantifiable categories. As we are constantly dealing with fluid concepts, we might decide to employ several observers/judges in order to check the consistency of classification – a type of 'double marking'.

Therefore, we can say that research is reliable if it is a consistent, rather than a rogue, finding. If people of the same class consistently vote for the same party then we may presume that the social and partisan alignment theory is reliable.

How do we ensure that our research is reliable? Shively (1998, pp. 41–42) identifies some common sources of unreliability in social science research:

1   *Varying sources* By using different samples of people we may produce very different results. We may decide to repeat a survey after a six-month break and uncover very different responses. However, this may be because we interviewed a completely different sample of people who hold very different opinions for genuine reasons. It is important for the British Election Panel Survey (see later), for example, to interview the same people over a period of time. If we wish to make observations about stability or changes in attitudes and opinions, it is important that we compare 'like with like'.

2   *Random errors* This can be simple replication errors or errors due to ambiguity. For example, if we are entering large amounts of data into a computer, we may on occasion hit the wrong key. Also, it is very important that the questions we ask are as unambiguous as possible. If we wanted to measure 'what party did you last vote for?' we might want to make this more precise by knowing how long ago that vote was cast, and in what level of election (a general election or local election for example).

3   *Problems with the research design* Such problems can derive from a variety of sources, and it is usual practice when designing survey-based research to employ a pilot study (see Chapter 3) in order to eradicate these sources of unreliability. It is important, for example, that we eradicate potential *errors of understanding*. Attitude measures can be unreliable if respondents do not understand the issue being analysed. There is little point in asking respondents to comment about the appropriateness of electoral reform if they have only a limited understanding of the system in operation and a similar appreciation of the alternatives available. We must also bear in mind that hypothetical questions tend to provoke hypothetical answers ('if you were to earn more than £50,000 would you be more or less likely to vote for Party X?'). It is very important that the people we are studying have some knowledge and appreciation of the topic we are researching.

      Reliability errors can also derive from *badly phrased questions*. In particular, we should avoid using double negatives and implying characteristics, such as: 'Will William Hague's inability to manage his party make the Conservatives unelectable?' People may not feel that William Hague has any difficulty in managing the Conservative Party, but might feel that this party is unelectable for other reasons.

4   *Problems in the process of data collection* Despite our best attempts to prepare for our research, we may encounter problems when we are in the process of data collection. One potential source of unreliability is *interviewer/respondent effects*. Respondents may feel that they have no reason to 'play the game' and may tell the interviewer blatant lies. Alternatively, dishonest interviewers play games with the researcher by filling in forms themselves. *Respondent replies may vary with their mood*. For example, a person's attitude towards public transport policy may be affected because their train was late. Attitudes towards political parties can be affected by scandals which appear in the news. This may particularly be the case for issues on which respondents do not have strong

feelings or levels of interest. Alternatively, we might encounter expectancy and modelling effects. Respondents may feel there is a 'right' answer and may look for 'cues' from the interviewer.

The problems encountered when trying to establish reliability are highlighted by an American survey which interviewed the same respondents after a two-year interval. On average, the respondents reported being a different gender on 0.5 per cent of occasions, whereas their race did not change at all. More importantly, respondents reported a lower educational background than their previous response on average 13 per cent of the time, which is logically impossible (Shively, 1998, p. 42).

Therefore, there are steps we can take to try to reduce unreliability. We can eliminate clerical errors by double-checking. We can use pilot studies to eliminate ambiguous questions. In some cases, we can retest respondents after a set period of time. This works better for factual questions (how did you vote in last election?) than attitudes (respect for a party leader), and thus we must appreciate that attitudinal surveys are particularly vulnerable to potential unreliability.

Validity is 'the extent to which our measures correspond to the concepts they are intended to reflect' (Mannheim and Rich, 1995, p. 73). The measure must be both appropriate and complete. Let us look at the example of 'political activity'. It would not be appropriate to use trade union membership as a measure of political activity, as people join trade unions for a variety of (often non-political) reasons. It would be more appropriate to use measures such as writing to an MP or voting – we can see that these are clear forms of political activity. However, they may be insubstantial measures on their own. If we were to say that anyone who has either not written to their MP or has not voted is 'politically inactive' we would be defining political activity in a rather narrow (and invalid) way. A complete measure of political activity may also include behaviour such as standing for an election; donating money to a cause; signing a petition; and taking part in a demonstration.

Black (1993, pp. 168–172) identifies *types* of validity:

1   *Construct validity*   This is an important issue in research design, as we are often measuring abstract traits such as social class or party identification. We must be clear about the meaning of the terminology that we use. Problems with terminology may include concepts such as 'unemployed' – are students and housewives unemployed? If we are testing attitudes towards 'a party's ability to govern', we need to decide how this can be measured. For example, we might decide to measure perceptions concerning a range of policies and issues, but also to measure attitudes regarding leadership strength. Therefore, construct validity is the degree to which a measurement actually measures the identified concept for which it is intended (Keman, in Pennings *et al.*, 1999, p. 86).

2   *Content validity*   We need to ensure that we reflect the range of the subject. For example, in order to establish party preference we should ask questions about all, not just one or two, parties. An interesting example of the challenges we may face in ensuring research validity is demonstrated by the *Literary Digest* presidential election polls carried out in the United States. These polls were carried out in the 1920s and 1930s, and consisted of postal questionnaires which

had a response rate of 20 per cent. Despite the low response rate, the *Literary Digest* successfully predicted the outcome of several elections with a fair degree of accuracy, but failed to do so in 1936. The reason? The fundamental flaw lay in the representativeness of the sample. Questionnaires were sent to those who were registered as car and/or telephone owners (which was heavily class influenced at that time). The representativeness of the survey was then further undermined by the fact that successful completion of the survey required self-motivation, and thus 'after 1936, the sympathies of the middle class were no longer a valid measure of the way the country would vote' (Shively, 1998, p. 47).

Problems with measuring political variables: a summary

To summarise the concerns we have raised so far: despite the many advantages of using numerical analysis in order to explain political behaviour and events, we nevertheless need to consider the weaknesses, constraints and problems encountered when employing such methods.

The first problem we have focused upon relates to the of accuracy of terminology. As political science relies so heavily upon multidimensional, subjective concepts we need to be very clear about what we are analysing. The simple example of 'votes cast in an election' is a good case – do we only include valid votes or do we include invalid votes as well? Unclear terminology will eventually affect the reliability of our research; someone carrying out the exact same study may get very different results if they use different definitions.

Yet there are also other sources of unreliability in political research. If we are dealing with large amounts of quantitative data there is the possibility of clerical errors being made. We can demonstrate this by looking at a section of Table 2.1. Our quantitative research can also be undermined by a lack of precision. This may be a problem when assessing social class. Precision can be affected in two ways: first, we have a large amount of information to input, and we may put the same occupation into different groups during different input sessions; second, we may come across, say, an occupation that does not match our expected list, and probably cannot return to the respondent for greater clarification. Our decision, in a case like this, may be a fairly arbitrary one.

We need to appreciate that general levels of understanding of and interest in politics will vary, and as a result we might encounter an 'understanding gap'. This means that the same respondent may give a different response to the same question at different times because they have little understanding/knowledge of the research topic, rather than because there has been a real change in attitude or opinion. What is the point of asking someone whether 'Quangos play a positive role in the democratic process?' if they do not know what a quango is? This would obviously undermine the validity of our research.

The problem of using complex political concepts is demonstrated by electoral studies. For example, psephologists are often interested in the impact of ideology on voting – but how should it be measured? We can ask respondents to place themselves on a left–right scale (the problem of using such a scale has already be identified – people may have different interpretations of where the centre lies). Alternatively, we

Table 2.1 Example of a clerical error

In relation to the 1983 General Election, the figures presented as the size of the electorate and the total number of votes are identical. This may lead us to believe that turnout was 100 per cent, or that a simple typing error has been made.

	Total votes	MPs elected	Candidates	Unopposed returns	% share of total vote	Vote per opposed candidate
1983 Thursday, 9 June						
Conservative	13,012,315	397	633	—	42.4	43.5
Liberal	4,210,115	17	322	—	13.7	27.7
Social Democrat	3,570,834	6	311	—	11.6	24.3
(Alliance)	(7,780,949)	(23)	(633)	—	(25.4)	(26.0)
Labour	8,456,934	209	633	—	27.6	28.3
Communist	11,606	—	35	—	0.04	0.8
Plaid Cymru	125,309	2	36	—	0.4	7.8
Scottish Nat. P.	331,975	2	72	—	1.1	11.8
National Front	27,065	—	60	—	0.1	1.0
Others (G.B.)	193,383	—	282	—	0.6	1.4
Others (N.I.)	764,925	17	95	—	3.1	17.9
Elec. 42,197,344 Turnout 72.7%	42,197,344	650	2,579	—	100.0	—

Source: Butler and Butler (1994, p. 219)

may ask a series of questions to make judgements about the respondent. Many agree that this latter method is more appropriate as: 'the more direct measures of left–right ideological position presuppose a degree of political understanding on the part of the respondents that may not in fact be warranted' (Sanders, 1999, p. 185). Hence, there is a recognition that an understanding gap may exist.

Using statistical analysis in political science

We have already discussed the fact that quantitative analysis involves different types, or qualities, of data, and as we progress from nominal to ratio level data we are dealing with a *higher quality* of information; that is, the data tell us more about the phenomena we are studying. However, data are of little use to us if we cannot *analyse* and *manipulate* them. Or to put it another way, 'it is not sufficient for social researchers to be merely literate; they must also be numerate' (Rose and Sullivan, 1993, p. 3).

We might use data analysis for two purposes: to analyse the data we collect ourselves (primary data), or to analyse the data collected by others (secondary data), for example, the BES data which is held in the Data Archive at the University of Essex. What can the data do? Well, in social science (and political science in particular) we do not prove findings or outcomes. Because we are inevitably involved in studying the attitudes and behaviours of individuals, these can change over time and between cases and we would be unwise to state that something *always* happens just because it occurred before. Even if we are studying institutions we are inevitably dealing with human interaction. Studies accounting for practices in the House of Commons are really studies of the actors within this institution (for example, Members of Parliament, political researchers, administration staff, lobby correspondents), rather than the physical features of the building. Therefore: 'data analysis is concerned with *explaining variance*, with explaining why there is variability in some particular characteristic in a population or sample which is of theoretical importance to social researchers' (Rose and Sullivan, 1993, p. 6) – thus, looking at how political activity and opinions change, to what extent change occurs, and how this impacts upon our existing knowledge and expectations of politics.

As the number of examples we are examining grows, we have to familiarise ourselves with techniques and procedures which enable us to *manage* the information; that is, we become increasingly reliant upon computers and their programs for data analysis. The first British Election Study carried out in 1963, for example, asked 2009 respondents a total of 85 questions – a total of 170,765 separate pieces of information (in fact, the real number of data was much greater as many questions involved sub-questions). What we have to bear in mind though is that data analysis provides only a means to an end – the results mean nothing if we cannot use the information to answer questions that we have derived from theory.

Types of analysis

Once we have collected our data we need to assess it, in order to make some assumptions and claims. Statistics present a limited amount of information, and in politics we are also interested in the relationship between *variables*. For example, in a survey we might find out that x per cent vote Labour and y per cent vote Conservative. However, what may be of more interest is the percentage of males and females in each category of voters. As such, we discuss voting behaviour as being a *dependent variable* that may be influenced by a range of factors, such as age, gender and class among other factors.

In order to identify relationships between variables, we can employ different levels of analysis, which range from the simple to the more complex.

Univariate analysis

This is simply asking the question 'how many' – be it the number of pressure group members or the size of civil service departments, for example. Within this level of analysis we include averages and distributions: we might find that people join more than one pressure group, or that they read more than one particular newspaper per week. Averages and distributions help us to make sense of data when we are studying a large number of cases; for example, what is the average age of party members? what is the average length of time people spend watching the daily news?

Bivariate analysis

This is the method we use when we want to compare variables to look for relationships, for example, the relationship between educational attainment and party support, or the relationship between political activity and newspaper readership. There is a range of statistical tests we can employ to identify whether *significant* (see the earlier explanation of what significant means in a research context) relationships exist. These include: cross-tabulation; scattergrams; correlations; regression analysis; and factor analysis (Miller, 1995, p. 159). However, just because a relationship exists, this does not necessarily mean that one variable causes the other. In Chapter 1 we touched upon the complex relationship between political communication and political partisanship – does newspaper readership influence party support, or do we read newspapers that are sympathetic towards our political leaning?

Multivariate analysis

This level of analysis is used to comprehend the relationship between three or more variables. For example, we might believe that class alone is not a sufficient indicator of voting behaviour and may also want to take into account a *whole range* of other factors (such as area of residency, car ownership and newspaper readership). Again, a range of statistical tests exists to test for significant relationships: multiple regression; interaction models; path analysis; and multiple factor models (Miller, 1995, p. 160).

This method of analysis was employed by Brand *et al.* (1994) in their study of Scottish National Party (SNP) voters. This study considered a range of social and political characteristics which were identified as being likely to result in a voter opting for the SNP. By using logistic regression analysis, the study was able to demonstrate that support for Scottish independence, strong Scottish national identification and age were more strongly linked to voting for the SNP than were class, religion, trade union membership or gender (Brand *et al.*, 1994, p. 618).

Time-series models

This approach is employed in order to analyse trends over time, for example, changes in economic performance, changes (or not) in public opinion. It is useful for understanding the length of time it takes for changes to occur. Due to the nature of time-scale analysis it tends to be wholly employed by those mapping (and also predicting) trends in party support (Miller, 1995, p. 164). Time-series analysis has been employed to study the impact of political events such as a change in party leadership, and the change in party support that occurred as a result of 'Black Wednesday' (see Clarke *et al.*, 1999 for an example).

Case studies of quantitative political analysis

Case study 1: SPSS

The aim of this section is to introduce you to one of the most frequently used methods of statistical analysis, SPSS. This is not a 'how to' guide *per se* – this is provided in texts elsewhere (Rose and Sullivan, 1993; Corston and Colman, 2000; Fielding and Gilbert, 2000) – but rather is an illustration of the reasons for using SPSS and its opportunities for analysis.

SPSS was launched in 1968 and initially represented the title 'Statistical Package for Social Sciences', although it has recently become the abbreviation for 'Statistical Product and Service Solutions' (Corston and Colman, 2000). The main point you need to know about SPSS is that it only works with information which is in numerical form. That means that once we have carried out our research we need to put the information into numerical (exclusive) categories. We enter the data for statistical analysis into a spreadsheet and place each individual response to the same question in the same column. Let us take some examples from the 1963 British Election Study to demonstrate how we might analyse our data via SPSS.

Q. 22 Would you like to see the death penalty kept?
This is a fairly straightforward question which requires a simple response. As SPSS does not recognise words, we need to be able to give each response a numerical code, and we might do this in the following way:

> *1 = yes*
> *2 = no*

When we come to enter the data from the completed questionnaires we might find that these two simple categories are not enough, they do not 'exhaust' the range of possible responses. We might find, for example, that some respondents replied ' don't know'. We therefore need a third code for this question:

> *3 = don't know*

Also, we might find that some respondents refused to answer the question (this is more likely to be the case with self-completion surveys than face-to-face surveys). For these respondents none of 'yes', 'no' or 'don't know' would be an appropriate code, and therefore a fourth code is required:

> *4 = no response*

You might now begin to appreciate that even relatively straightforward questions can take some time to code and analyse, and as the number of potential responses increases, so does the number of codes we need to exhaust all possible alternatives and thus carry out accurate statistical analysis (many researchers will tell you that the actual process of inputting data for analysis is very time consuming and very dull!).

Let us consider how we might code an open-ended question.

Q. 42 About how old were you when you first began to hear anything about politics?
The number of potential responses is obviously much broader than it was for the previous question. The nature of the question means that many respondents will give a broad response

(such as 'about six or seven'), although some may recall a particular event to which we can then give a specific date (such as the election of a new government or the declaration of war). Yet when it comes to analysing the responses, we might find it more useful to place them in broad categories. For example:

1 = less than 10 years of age
2 = 10–14 years of age
3 = 15–20 years of age
4 = 21 years or older

and not forgetting our categories for those who do not fit into one of the above:

5 = don't know
6 = no response

We do not have to have six codes for this question. We may want fewer codes (in which case we make the age groups broader) or we might want more codes (in which case we make the age groups smaller). This is a decision that political researchers must make for themselves. It is important to bear in mind though that whatever categories we use they should be 'exclusive' – that is, a response can fit into one category and one category alone. However, by changing the number of categories we are ultimately influencing the *quality* of our analysis. It might be more useful to know that there are twice as many respondents in the 'less than 10 years of age' group than in the '15–20 years of age' group, than it is to know that 95 per cent of respondents were under 20 years of age when they first began to hear anything about politics. Therefore, we should not make decisions about the number of categories purely on the basis of ease alone. We should always be thinking about ways in which we can make data comparable, yet still maintain the detail of the information wherever possible.

Therefore, we can use SPSS to help us manage large amounts of data. Once we have (correctly) entered data, SPSS will work out a range of simple and more complex statistical analyses (for example, it can work out average values but also test for significant relationships). We can also use SPSS to present our information in a visual form, for example, via graphs and charts and scatterplots.

Case study 2: the British Election Studies

The British General Election Surveys (BES) and sister-study the British Election Panel Studies (BEPS) are perhaps the most detailed and informative source of data which exist in relation to British General Elections – indeed, the BES constitute 'the longest series of academic surveys in Britain' (Taylor and Thomson, 1999, p. 272). The BES have been carried out after every General Election since 1964, and the BEPS since the 1992 General Election (although other panel surveys have previously been conducted). The data produced have also been supported by similar, related studies, such as the Scottish and Welsh studies and an Ethnic Minority Survey. The interviews are conducted on a face-to-face, rather than postal or telephone, basis (the exception was a postal referendum study in 1975), reinforcing the point made earlier in this chapter that volunteer sampling is not always ideal. All data from the BES studies are openly available from the ESRC Data Archive at the University of Essex.

BEPS constitute a *time-series* method of analysis, that is to say, a cross-section of people are interviewed at several points, or 'waves', between one election and the next. So, for example, members of the 1992 BEPS study were interviewed eight times, beginning just after the 1992 General Election and ending just after the 1997 General Election. The advantage of this approach is that it helps us to understand the extent to which *the same people* retain or change their attitudes and opinions over a lengthy period of time.

Prior to the initial BES study, knowledge about voting behaviour in Britain was largely gleaned from the candidates and parties themselves (Butler and Stokes, 1971, p. 26). It was not until the development and use of opinion polls in America in the 1930s that lessons regarding the *systematic* analysis of voters could be learnt. The systematic study of British General Elections was initiated in 1945 by R.B. McCallum and became synonymous with the Nuffield Studies. These studies relied upon three main sources of information: evidence from politicians and the media; evidence from opinion polls; and evidence from the actual results, although this did not give enough valuable insight into the motivations of the individual voter. The earliest studies of voting behaviour in Britain inevitably contained weaknesses:

> Their approach . . . tended to be confined by established sociological categories; they sought to find relationships between voting behaviour and class or sex or age or newspaper readership. But they did not go very far in exploring the reasons for these relationships or for the exceptions to them.
>
> (Butler and Stokes, 1971, p. 28)

As a result, the BES are largely created by, and for, academic purposes, although the dissemination of their findings spreads well beyond this remit. The series was originated by David Butler and Donald Stokes (British and American academics respectively), who sought to learn from the experiences of the Survey Research Center at the University of Michigan.

If we consider the first BES, Butler and Stokes opted to carry out a large-scale survey with two contact points: one before the official election campaign began and one directly after a general election. The first survey was carried out between 24 May and 13 August 1963, with 2009 randomly selected electors in England, Scotland and Wales. A similar size sample (1830) was contacted after the election between 18 October and 4 December 1964, and consisted of those who responded on the first occasion where possible, plus some additional new respondents. The third round of surveys took place just after the 1966 General Election (between 4 April and 4 June 1966 with a sample of 2086 respondents). Thus, participants were interviewed between one and three times.

Butler and Stokes (1971, p. 541) stress the importance of maintaining high and consistent response rates, claiming that:

> as the fraction [of those in the required sample but not interviewed] increases the possibility of serious bias must always be considered. If the persons who have not granted an interview differ from those who have, and if they constitute a substantial part of the whole, the findings obtained from the part of the sample interviewed will not be fully representative.

Earlier in this chapter we began to consider the issue of research populations and research samples. Butler and Stokes discuss the issue of *sampling error* in their text, suggesting that errors can arise, not necessarily due to the process of sampling, but because of an inability to make contact with those one would wish to study or because respondents may give 'misleading answers' (p. 547).

If we consider the most recent study in this series, the 1997 survey was conducted between 2 May (the day after the election) and 1 August, although the vast majority of surveys (96 per cent) had been completed by the end of June. The 1997 BES survey strove to analyse a 'representative sample of the population' in Britain who were over 18 and living in private households. Previously, the electoral register had been used to draw a sample, but this has become problematic. The aggregate number on the electoral register began to decline in 1989 due to the implementation of the Community Charge (Poll Tax). This in itself may not be problematic, although research has shown that those who did not register on the electoral roll were likely to be 'young, poor, mobile and ethnic minority citizens' (McLean and Smith, 1995, p. 144) who were more likely to support the Labour or Liberal Democrat parties than the Conservative Party. This sampling method has now been replaced by a multi-stage design which identifies households by postcodes and delivery points (see Taylor and Thomson, 1999, pp. 273–275, for a more detailed explanation of the sampling frame). The BES survey itself consisted of two parts: the first part was carried out as a face-to-face interview (taking an average of just over one hour to complete); and the second part consisted of a self-completion questionnaire (completed by 86 per cent of respondents). The use of the self-completion supplement has been in place since the 1987 election and exists to increase the number of questions that can be asked. However, it also includes a set of questions on attitudes towards democratic institutions and processes which form part of the Comparative Study of Electoral Systems. These questions will also be employed in election studies in numerous other countries to enable comparative analysis. The data created by each of the BES have provided a wealth of information on long-term voting practices and hold a central place in the process of political analysis.

Conclusion

This chapter has drawn attention to some of the issues and concerns which we should consider when embarking upon quantitative political analysis. The often subjective and multidimensional nature of what we study as political scientists serves to make quantitative analysis often complex and certainly imperfect. This should not, however, deter us from using such research tools, and indeed great advances have been made in order to make our studies more scientific and precise.

The purpose of this chapter is not to suggest that there is a universal 'right' way of conducting quantitative political research, but rather to draw attention to the type of information we can study, the methods of analysis we can employ, and the pitfalls we need to recognise if we are to generate reliable and valid studies. As Keman suggests, the search for objective knowledge 'is a dream situation in social sciences', yet this should not prevent us from producing studies which are 'value free' (in Pennings *et al.*, 1999, p. 5).

Further reading

Quantitative political analysis is dealt with on an introductory level in W.P. Shively, *The Craft of Political Research*, 4th edn, Englewood Cliffs, NJ: Prentice-Hall, 1998; and J.B. Mannheim and R.C. Rich, *Empirical Political Analysis*, 4th edn, New York: Longman, 1995.

For those who are more comfortable working with statistical formulae, I suggest paying further attention to P. Pennings *et al.*, *Doing Research in Political Science*, London: Sage, 1999 (in particular, Part II); or R.A. Bernstein and J.A. Dyer, *An Introduction to Political Science Methods*, 3rd edn, Englewood Cliffs, NJ: Prentice-Hall, 1992.

In relation to sampling techniques, Chapter 10 in J. Fielding and N. Gilbert *Understanding Social Statistics*, London: Sage, 2000, is easy to follow. Schofield's chapter, entitled 'Survey sampling', in R. Sapsford and V. Jupp (eds), *Data Collection and Analysis*, London: Sage, 1996, is also useful.

For those who require a practical guide to using SPSS, I recommend D. Rose and O. Sullivan, *Introducing Data Analysis for Social Scientists*, Buckingham: Open University Press, 1993; R. Corston and A. Colman, *A Crash Course in SPSS for Windows*, Oxford: Blackwell, 2000 and J. Fielding and N. Gilbert, *Understanding Social Statistics*, London: Sage, 2000.

Chapter 3

Using surveys in political research

Introduction

In this chapter we shall consider the role that surveys and questionnaires have to play in political research. If we want to find out about political attitudes, and we want to know about a group of people rather than just a small number of individuals, we are likely at some point in our research to make use of survey data (which we may have collected ourselves or which may have been collected by others). The founding fathers of social research surveys in Britain were Charles Booth and Seebohm Rowntree (with their studies of poverty commencing in the late nineteenth century) and A.L. Bowley's study of working-class conditions which began in 1912 (Broughton, 1995, p. 3). The development of research tools such as sampling (see Chapter 2) allowed researchers to progress beyond the need for exhaustive surveys (Fielding and Gilbert, 2000, p. 225).

In this chapter we shall consider the advantages and disadvantages of using surveys and pay attention to some of the methodological considerations that you will need to appreciate if you are to carry out your own surveys. To carry out your survey properly is a very large undertaking and should not be attempted unless you are sure that the resources are in place. The following section of this chapter will analyse the contribution of opinion polling to political research. The validity of opinion polls in political research became a particularly contentious issue after the 1992 General Election: we shall consider why this was the case and what has been done to rectify potential weaknesses.

We have already touched upon some of the issues relevant to survey-based research in previous chapters. For example, in Chapter 1 we identified the contribution of surveys to the development of the behavioural approach in the 1930s. In Chapter 2 we introduced the idea of 'measuring' political concepts and attitudes – focusing upon the importance of clarity of definition and common understandings – particularly if we want to compare research findings. We introduced the concept of research populations and differing types of research samples: the way in which we select a survey sample requires serious consideration, not least because the quality of the sample will influence the quality of the research. We also discussed the notion of research reliability and validity, and looked at some examples of how research may undermine these principles. In this chapter we concentrate upon the issues and concerns which you might face when constructing and operationalising your own survey-based political research.

What is a survey?

The use of *questionnaires* and *surveys* in political research is associated with the generation of quantitative data, and they are most commonly employed in the real world within the field of market research (which has both a political and a non-political remit). In comparison to some of the research techniques we will consider in Part II of this text (for example, qualitative interviews), surveys can act as a rapid and relatively cheap method of questioning populations. That is not to imply that they are 'easy', as the preparation and the design are pivotal. In political research, we employ questionnaires to explore research questions which cover 'personal experiences, perceptions, opinions, attitudes and reported behaviors of still-living persons' (Kleinnjenhuiis, in Pennings *et al.*, 1999, p. 78). What is the difference between a questionnaire and a survey? A questionnaire is the means by which we implement a survey. The list of questions we ask forms the basis of the questionnaire, whilst the results we gather (whether from 50, 100 or 1000+ respondents) and the analysis we carry out form the survey. Surveys are standardised in the way they are administered, the questions are asked in the same order and are scored in the same way.

Surveys cannot tell us everything there is to know about political phenomena, and in Part II we shall consider methods of acquiring qualitative data. Surveys are, however, very useful for finding out five types of information about respondents (see Briefing box 3.1). For example, detailed survey research of Labour Party members has examined the changing patterns of political activity. By providing respondents with a list of activities, Whiteley and Seyd (1998) have been able to identify differences between old and new members.

In politics, survey methods are most frequently used to test opinion towards certain policies and to track the patterns of party preference during election campaigns. The means by which we gather survey data vary considerably. We might, for example, conduct face-to-face surveys in which an interviewer reads out a list of questions and writes down the verbal response. Market research surveys are increasingly being carried out over the telephone, or take the form of self-completion (the problems of these different approaches were discussed in Chapter 2). Surveys which rely upon technological access can produce quirky and often bizarre results. Many 'millennium polls' were carried out in 1999 which provided some 'interesting' outcomes:

> During one BBC News Online poll, after unusual voting patterns were detected, on exasperated spokesman said: 'We just can't accept any more votes for Miss Piggy.' ... *Time* magazine smelt a rat in August when for 12 hours Ronnie O'Brien, a 20-year-old Irish footballer and Middlesbrough FC reject, topped its 'person of the century' internet poll ... Soon after the *Time* poll was launched,

---

Briefing box 3.1 Types of information acquired by survey research

- Facts – where respondents live, their age, their academic qualifications.
- Perceptions – what people know about the world (we might ask respondents to name their local MP or to identify members of the Cabinet).
- Opinions – what people think about the world (judgements about the competencies of political party leaders).
- Attitudes – these are relatively stable evaluations (support for wealth distribution, antipathy towards bloodsports).
- Behavioural reports – how people act (does the respondent read a newspaper, does he/she vote in general elections?).

Source: Mannheim and Rich (1995, p. 129)

Adolf Hitler became a frontrunner amid suspicions of massive electronic voting from Nazi groups.

(Smith and Barot, 2000)

Whilst we cannot force people to participate in surveys against their will, we do need to be constantly aware of the reasons why some people may be more willing than others to respond to a questionnaire. We may be able to address this concern by focusing our survey towards different types of respondents. We can distinguish between *mass surveys*, in which we are interested in the responses of the general population, and *elite surveys*, where we are 'interviewing people who are defined by their position as being important in some way' (Bernstein and Dyer, 1992, p. 91). As such, they have particular knowledge which is central to the survey; an elite survey may be one which focuses upon MPs, civil servants or pressure group personnel.

As we mentioned in the introduction, survey research, when conducted appropriately, is a considerable undertaking, and the qualities of speed and cost are comparative ones. Never assume that survey research is easy (see Briefing box 3.2).

It is vital when carrying out survey work that we pre-plan, and indeed it is often the case that we invest a great deal of time and energy in what we term pre-testing, or *pilot studies*. Imagine that a sponsor has given you a large amount of money to survey opinions about legislation reform, and they are particularly interested in discovering whether people favour a ban on bloodsports. After carrying out the survey, you find that the survey has attracted a large number of refusals, or that due to complex and technical language, respondents could not answer the questions accurately. Your sponsor will not be very happy with either of these outcomes, and further research sponsorship is unlikely to materialise.

Briefing box 3.2 Considerations in survey design

An appropriate survey should:

- reflect relevant theoretical propositions in its construction;
- use results from the sample to generalise about the population;
- be replicable.

To design a good questionnaire one should:

- read around the topic;
- decide on the aims;
- decide the population and sample groups;
- pilot the work to be undertaken.

Source: Adapted from May (1993, pp. 67–83)

Hence, we carry out pilot studies with a small number of respondents to check that questions are not ambiguous and do not provoke unexpected interpretations. The author's own experience shows that questions can be easily misinterpreted. A survey was carried out in 1997 among sixth formers to analyse levels of political interest and political participation. The researchers originally included a question which asked: 'What is the main difference between the three main parties?' One respondent replied: 'Red, blue and yellow' (referring to the colours associated with the Labour Party, the Conservative Party and the Liberal Democrats). This was not the kind of response we had anticipated, and this question was removed from further surveys. Therefore, careful consideration should be given to the construction of surveys, and in relation to research that you may carry out as part of your own studies, 'using questions that have been used in surveys that have a proven record of utility and acceptance is usually better than constructing new questions' (Bernstein and Dyer, 1992, p. 94).

The advantages of employing survey research

We should not underestimate the significant role that surveys have played in developing our understanding of political attitudes and behaviour. The obvious advantages lie in their cost and breadth. Financially, surveys may not be cheap – we have to think about how much it takes to print surveys, whether we need to include postage or telephone costs, and whether we need to employ interviewers to collect the data. All these costs will increase as we study larger samples of the research population. Yet the financial outlay is often compensated for by the time taken to carry out surveys. It is possible to draft a survey quickly (bearing in mind that we need to carry out a pilot study); this is particularly useful if we wish to research a topical issue (for example, a survey to measure the popularity of the candidates standing for London mayor is not much use after the election has been held). Also, because surveys ask a limited number of questions which will have short, often restricted, responses we can analyse the findings fairly swiftly (especially with the help of computer programs). Analysing long interviews is far more time consuming. In relation to breadth, we can survey far more respondents than we can realistically hope to interview in-depth. A survey may take about 10–30 minutes to complete, whereas an in-depth interview can often take more than an hour (not to mention the time it takes to actually set up the interview).

Surveys may offer a feasible alternative to interviews if we are dealing with sensitive or contentious political issues. For example, during the course of researching the attitudes of Conservative MPs towards the Maastricht Treaty, Blair (1999, p. 119) found that the sensitivity of the issue:

> limited the number of individuals who were willing to be interviewed because they did not want to deepen divide within the Party. Second, those who were central to the negotiation of the Treaty were still in government, and many still in Cabinet.

In contrast, surveys obtained similar types of information for Blair, but helped to ensure anonymity, potentially increasing participation rates.

Yet to assume that all surveys are the same is not appropriate. Surveys can take different formats, and this inevitably affects the 'richness' and usefulness of the information we collect. Mannheim and Rich identify two general survey formats:

1   *Cross sectional surveys*   We ask our respondents to complete the survey on one occasion only, and as such these surveys provide 'a snapshot of a moving target' (Mannheim and Rich, 1995, p. 132). We must recognise that, particularly in relation to political attitudes, the responses we gain might be very different if we had conducted the survey at an earlier or a later date.

2   *Longitudinal surveys*   For this approach we survey respondents on more than one occasion to look for stability or changes in attitudes and opinions. This may be achieved via *trend surveys*, in which we survey different people from the same population (for example, a trend survey of members of a political party might want to find out the reasons why new members join the party). *Cohort*, or *panel*, *surveys* focus upon the same sample of people over a period of time (see the example of the British Election Panel Studies discussed in Chapter 2) in order to measure changes in opinions.

The disadvantages of employing survey research

Whilst there are undoubtedly many benefits to using surveys in political research, we can identify several potential problems. First, we may encounter a poor response rate, or we may have wider worries about the appropriateness of the samples surveyed. Second, it may be an inappropriate tool for the subject matter. The responses may not be 'genuine' but rather reflect the expectations of the survey. We shall not elaborate upon sampling and response rates here, as this has already been discussed in Chapter 2. There are, however, potential problems with longitudinal panel surveys, for example, in that this approach can make the research expensive and may lead to the effect of *reactivity*: 'the reaction of human subjects to the knowledge that they are being investigated' (Wilson, 1996, p. 95). For example, respondents actually become more interested and more knowledgeable about a topic because they know they are going to be surveyed again; or inaccurate responses are compounded by people's attitudes being fundamentally changed by being forced to consider the same questions repeatedly. If, for example, we were to conduct a survey which asks people's opinions on Party X and the issue of sleaze, we may reach the stage where respondents begin to link the two concepts (when previously they did not). The problem of reactivity can potentially raise ethical issues if we are dealing with a controversial topic. Furthermore, panel surveys may be subject to attrition, where people drop out of the study (they might become fed-up with repeatedly being surveyed, they may move and become uncontactable, or they may die), and this might affect the study's representativeness (Mannheim and Rich, 1995, p. 133).

Dunleavy (1990) has identified two shortcomings of using the survey method to study mass political behaviour. He draws attention to a resources issue, whereby 'a reputable survey' requires substantial financial support, and to a structural issue – 'how questions are phrased is of the first importance to the ways in which they can subsequently be analysed' (p. 457) – both of which may contribute to these shortcomings. First, British election studies have ignored context, such as the importance of neighbourhood, socialisation processes and local politics, although studies carried out since the early 1990s have begun to address this omission. Second, single-response questions are not sufficient as the meaning, or context, of responses can change over time. The problem here lies in the fact that the same terms can have different meanings over time, and 'asked over several decades . . . the meaning of responses to questions . . . becomes completely indeterminate' (ibid.). As such, we can end up classifying together people with quite dissimilar views because the question wording has become decontextualised. A possible solution to the problem is to replace single-response items with batteries of questions in which people can be classed in terms of the consistency or mixture of their multiple responses (ibid.). Therefore, Dunleavy's point is that surveys provide only limited information, and we should not necessarily expect too much from the type of rather superficial data that surveys collect (rather we should use various analytical methods if possible).

Another, more particular, problem is that surveys may be attempting to measure something which is not easy to discover. For many people, politics may not be a predominant concern and by carrying out a survey we are trying to measure quickly attitudes and opinions which have not been given much serious consideration. We need to pay attention to survey format to ensure that we gain reliable answers. Bernstein and Dyer (1992, p. 95) point out that 'some questions may influence the responses to other questions on the same questionnaire'. This may particularly be the case if we include scales in our survey. A respondent may, for example, feel that he or she approves of a particular policy (such as spending on education), but what is the exact difference between '*agreeing some of the time*' and '*agreeing most of the time*'? Again, we may find we are in the situation where we are asking respondents to classify themselves in a sense that is not usually a consideration. The difference between 'some of the time' and 'most of the time' is subjective rather than concrete. Scales are, therefore, perhaps most useful when seeking out factual information. If the respondent has little motivation to be honest (or does not really care about the subject matter), we may experience what is referred to as *response set*: 'when a series of questions are asked in the same form; this encourages respondents to mark them all the same way, regardless of the substance of the questions' (Bernstein and Dyer, 1992, p. 95). In surveys carried out in 1994, it was found that more people reported that they were 'certain to vote' in the European election of that year than actually did vote (Broughton, 1995, p. 46).

The effects of questionnaire design are explored by Bartle (1999), who suggests that the British Election Studies questionnaire might encourage respondents to give the same response to the questions on reported vote and party identification because the latter immediately follows the former. As a result, people who do not consider themselves as identifiers with a party will report identifying with the party they currently prefer, 'thus inflating the strength of relationship between party identification and vote' (p. 123). If you do choose to operationalise a survey, you will do well to take the advice of Swetnam (1995, p. 49): 'Try to see the questionnaire from the recipient's point of view. Are they likely to be interested in it or co-operative? How could they be encouraged?'

Methodological issues

Once we have decided that a survey is an appropriate means of gathering political data, we need to deal with the methodological concerns which can often undermine the rigour of our research. The first concern we shall face is who or what do we want to research? It is important that we have some awareness of our target population before we even begin to design the survey (as it may influence the language that we use). Closely tied to this is the decision we have to make about sampling, as 'we almost never look at all of the units in the theoretical population' (Bernstein and Dyer, 1992, p. 37). Sapsford and Abbott (1996) point to the fact that very few of the major British mobility surveys have paid much attention to women. Obviously, the representativeness of our sample affects the accuracy of statistical probability theory.

We have already mentioned that the sample we survey will be influenced by costs, but we also have to consider availability – it might be very interesting to find out about the first generation of women voters, but how many are we likely to find and be able to survey? Remember, we stated in Chapter 2 that the bigger our sample, the greater the chance that our observations are correct, *if* we are able to research representative samples: do not be mislead into thinking that a survey of 2000 is going to be any more accurate than a survey of 200 if we are relying upon probability sampling.

Once we have decided upon our target sample, we then need to construct an appropriate survey. We have already discussed in Chapter 2 some of the common sources of inaccurate responses to research questions. For example, using complex terminology or asking leading questions. We must bear in mind that politics is a very personal topic to many people and we should avoid asking sensitive questions. Existing research has shown that wording can be important. For example, different responses may be elicited if we ask 'Which party is better at creating job opportunities?' than if we ask 'Which party is better at dealing with unemployment?'.

We must also give some consideration to the types of response we require. Do we wish to ask *closed questions*, in which we provide respondents with a list of responses and ask them to pick the most appropriate, or do we ask *open-ended questions*, in which we 'allow respondents to answer in their own words' (Mannhein and Rich, 1995, p. 135)? Closed questions make comparison easy, whilst open-ended questions may allow unanticipated answers to emerge. However, if we choose to ask open-ended questions, we must pay strict attention to consistency when analysing the answers. A study of sixth-formers and their political attitudes asked respondents: '*Which issues are dominant in British politics in the 1990s?*' As respondents were free to write down as many issues as they felt appropriate, the researchers had the responsibility of grouping together similar responses to produce meaningful analyses. Hence, the researcher-labelled category 'Europe' covered responses such as 'the single currency' and 'European relations' (Harrison and Deicke, 2000).

If we choose to employ 'closed questions', it is important that we are aware of and anticipate the range of responses that we may encounter. As part of their research into party members, Whiteley and Seyd (1998) provided respondents with a list of activities in order to assess levels of political activism. However, the list of activities can vary, depending upon the timing of the research. For example, a survey of Labour

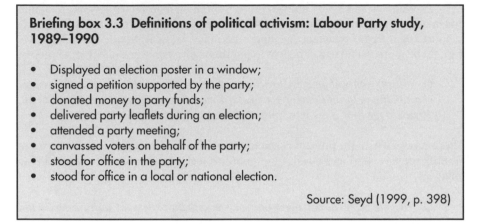

Briefing box 3.3 Definitions of political activism: Labour Party study, 1989–1990

- Displayed an election poster in a window;
- signed a petition supported by the party;
- donated money to party funds;
- delivered party leaflets during an election;
- attended a party meeting;
- canvassed voters on behalf of the party;
- stood for office in the party;
- stood for office in a local or national election.

Source: Seyd (1999, p. 398)

Party members carried out between 1989 and 1990 assessed political activism in terms of the activities outlined in Briefing box 3.3.

Respondents were asked to rate how often they had carried out such activities in terms of the following categories: *not at all*, *rarely*, *occasionally* and *frequently*. A similar survey was carried out after the 1997 General Election. On this occasion, the number of activities was expanded to take into account behaviour which we might only associate with the occurrence of elections (see Briefing box 3.4). This time, respondents were asked to rate themselves in relation to the categories: *not at all*, *once*, *twice* and *3+ occasions*.

Briefing box 3.4 Definitions of political activism: Labour Party study, 1997

- Displayed an election poster in a window;
- donated money to party funds;
- helped to run an election day committee room;
- drove voters to the polling station;
- took numbers at a polling station;
- reminded voters to vote;
- attended a vote count;
- canvassed voters (by phone or door-to-door);
- signed a petition supported by the party;
- helped with a fund-raising event;
- delivered party leaflets;
- attended a party meeting;
- attended a party rally;
- helped to organise a street stall;
- helped with mailings;
- helped with telephone fund-raising.

Source: Seyd (1999, p. 400)

As Whiteley and Seyd's studies show, a common method we may use to obtain information is to provide respondents with scales (which, as we stated earlier, may be more appropriate for factual questions). As many political attitudes are subjective, it might be more useful to ask people to put themselves on a scale. For example:

> Q. *Placing yourself on a scale between 1 and 10, how important is the gender of a candidate in influencing your vote; 1 would mean it is not important at all, 10 would mean it is the most important issue in deciding how to vote.*

Alternatively, we might present respondents with a *Likert scale*, which helps us to identify the direction and strength of people's feelings. An example would be as follows:

> Q. *To what extent do you agree or disagree with the statement 'foxhunting should be banned'?*
> strongly agree   agree   disagree   strongly disagree

However, we have already suggested that there may be some subjective distinction between the labels 'agree' and 'strongly agree', and we may decide that the direction of the opinion is more reliable than the strength of opinion *per se*.

Our final concern is to ensure that we actually get our (hopefully representative) sample to respond to our survey. It is unlikely that we will get a 100 per cent response rate to a large-scale survey, and there are some generally accepted standards when conducting social science research. For example, face-to-face surveys should have a response rate between 60 per cent and 85 per cent. Telephone surveys may have a slightly lower response rate as respondents are more likely to terminate a survey by putting down the phone than they are to walk away in a face-to-face situation. Self-completion and mail questionnaires inevitably have a lower response rate as they require some motivation to participate. (Seyd and Whiteley's studies have had relatively high response rates – 62.5 per cent in 1990 and 62.9 per cent in 1997. In comparison Wring *et al.*'s (1999) study of first-time voters had a response rate of 32 per cent.) Therefore, despite our best attempts to establish a representative sample, this may be undermined by the actual responses. Unfortunately, there is no guaranteed way of ensuring a sample response (perhaps except for the incentive of a large amount of money, but that is not particularly practical!), but we should be aware of factors which may influence propensity to participate in a study. For example, the demeanour of the interviewer may put off potential participants. American professional survey organisations prefer to employ middle-aged women as interviewers because respondents do not find them intimidating (Mannheim and Rich, 1995, p. 160). The timing of the survey may be relevant: if we carry out our survey by telephone, we need to be aware that different people will be at home at different times, whilst a mail survey may have a better response rate if it contains a stamped addressed envelope (Bernstein and Dyer, 1992, pp. 96–99).

Making use of opinion polls in political research

The concept of 'public opinion' is not as easy to define as it may sound – indeed Lippmann's study in 1922 claimed that in relation to the study of politics, 'the public' were neither knowledgeable nor competent enough to decide on matters of public policy (Broughton, 1995, p. 16). Broughton states that public opinion can be measured in terms of four dimensions:

1   *Intensity*   The strength of opinion. This tends to be strong on moral issues, for example, abortion, but weak on others (such as attitudes towards the European Union – see below).
2   *Stability*   Trends in public opinion tend to change over time, usually in a policy area which reflects generally limited knowledge, such as electoral reform. If we agree with Lippmann, we need to appreciate that the general public tends to have a limited understanding of many issues of public policy.
3   *Salience*   This is linked to the idea of issue stability, and relates to how an issue affects a person. For example, voters will be more likely to have an opinion on the funding of public transport if they travel to work by bus, tube or tram, and are more likely to be interested in education funding if they have young children. Hence issues surrounding foreign policy tend to have low saliency until periods of conflict.
4   *Latency*   This is an underlying opinion which is derived from other more direct response statements. For example, opinion on the issuing of identity cards may change after a spate of riots and public unrest.

The profile of opinion polls has increased as the process of electoral dealignment has led to a rise in the number of so-called floating voters. We should bear in mind two central concerns when looking at the use of opinion polls: the issues of sampling and of terminology (Moon, 1999, p. 24).

The problem with defining public opinion is that there is no typical person on the street, and so locating representative samples can be a complex task. Generally speaking, two methods are used: systematic probability sampling (the nth person on the electoral register) and quota sampling. In terms of polling voting intentions, the sample categories used include car ownership, housing tenure and political party supported (Moon, 1999, p. 31). A second problem is that polls only represent opinion at the time that they are taken – particularly on 'unstable' issues such as government popularity. Other problems include the fact that opinion polls cannot establish causal relationships. They may not be able to take into account the context of a person's beliefs. We can relate this to the earlier comment made in relation to Dunleavy's concerns. Simply replicating earlier survey questionnaires does not necessarily reflect the fact that the real-life political scenario has changed. We may, for example, find that there is a decline in the number of people 'concerned about crime'. This could be because the real crime figures have declined; because respondents feel that the positive action to deal with crime has improved; or simply because other concerns have become more important. We may be able to address this problem by employing multidimensional scaling techniques of analysis, although the simplicity of design becomes overshadowed by increasing technical sophistication.

Finally, opinion polls cannot directly measure complex political concepts, such as political alienation (Broughton, 1995, p. 25). Therefore, we cannot escape the fact that:

> The need to get the data collected and analysed quickly means that polls contain questions which cannot dig very deeply into the psyche of the ordinary voter and they are rarely detailed enough to untangle ideas of cause and effect.
>
> (Ibid., p. 88)

The development of opinion polling in Britain

The development of political opinion polls has gone hand in hand with the expansion of the franchise (Moon, 1999, p. 3). In Chapter 2 we considered the case of the 1936 *Literary Digest* presidential poll which predicted the wrong result because its sample was unrepresentative. Gallup began asking questions in Britain about 'satisfaction with the Prime Minister' in 1938, and the question: 'If there was an election tomorrow, who would you vote for?' in 1939 (Broughton, 1995, p. 4).

There is a ban on the reporting of opinion polls in some countries during the election period. This ranges from two days before the election in Canada, five days before the election in Spain, seven days before the election in France and Italy, and two weeks before the election in Portugal. A recommendation was made at the Speaker's Conference on Electoral Reform in 1967 that a pre-election poll ban of 72 hours should be implemented in Britain, but this has never been enforced (ibid., p. 7).

Broughton (1995) identifies several major developments in the industry of opinion polling since 1979. The first is the use of telephone polling: 90 per cent of British voters had phones in 1992, although nearly one-third were ex-directory. However, non-telephone owners are disproportionately poor and non-Conservative. Second, polling companies now make use of of computer-assisted telephone

---

Briefing box 3.5 Major polling firms in Britain

Polling company	*Year founded*
Gallup	1937 (1935 in USA)
National Opinion Polls (NOP)	1958
Harris	1965
Market and Opinion Research International (MORI)	1969
International Communications and Marketing (ICM)	1989

Source: Broughton (1995, p. 2)

---

interviewing (CATI) and computer-assisted personal interviewing (CAPI) for face-to-face interviews, which speeds up the process of data analysis. Third, we have witnessed an increase in the amount of secondary reporting of opinion poll results – inevitably leading to misinterpretation, and as Broughton (ibid., p. 12) says: 'The main danger emanates from the use that parties make of these exercises in their propaganda as a means of establishing the "likely" outcome of the election without explaining the purely hypothetical and conditional nature of the projection.'

Changing trends in British public opinion

Norris (1997b, pp. 164–170) considers the changing patterns and trends in public opinion which have been measured by the British Election Studies (BES) since 1964. In relation to support for the principles of privatisation and nationalisation, BES data showed that public opinion remained stable between 1964 and 1974, with a balance between those supporting continued nationalisation and those supporting increased privatisation. A shift in support towards privatisation appeared between 1974 and 1979, and as such the Conservative Party's drive to denationalise many major industries was in tune with the mood of the electorate. By 1992, the general feeling was that privatisation had gone far enough, and public opinion returned to its 1964 pattern.

In relation to trade unionism, the BES showed that trade unions were increasingly being perceived as too powerful from 1964 to 1974. Again, the Conservative Party's reforms reflected the tide of public opinion, and by 1992 fewer than one-third thought that the unions were too powerful. In comparison, Thatcherite policies on moral traditionalism were out of line with public opinion, as the period between 1974 and 1992 witnessed an increase in the liberalist approach, not a swing to the right. Hence, according to Norris, opinion polls demonstrated that the Conservative government captured the economic mood of the country but not the moral mood: there is no evidence to suggest that Thatcher successfully converted the electorate on the issues of strong government, discipline and free enterprise.

We mentioned earlier the concept of issues salience – that is, there are some topics which are more important to the public as a whole, and therefore that public opinion on these topics will remain more stable. An issue which appears to lack salience is Europe – or more precisely, Britain's membership of the European Union. Flickinger (1995, p. 199) suggests that this is an issue marked 'by sharp differences of view and considerable volatility', and his study has shown that party attachment plays a significant role in influencing public opinion towards the EU, whereas there is little evidence that attitudes towards the EU influence voting behaviour.

Case study: the mixed fortunes of opinion polling in political analysis

Opinion polling at election time: the débâcle of 1992 and the lessons learnt

To be fair, opinion polling during and preceding campaigns is not intended to predict results, although final polls and exit polls are. Opinion polls are employed in between elections to measure the popularity of policies and party leaders, and have been used to prompt political decisions (for example, the Conservative leader Sir Alec Douglas-Home decided to stand down as party leader in 1965 after poor popularity reports, and Harold Wilson called the 1966 General Election on the back of positive poll findings; see Broughton, 1995, p. 7). Added to the public polls, much private polling has been undertaken by the parties since the 1960s to test out policy proposals and advertising campaigns, although the results of these are usually kept under close wraps by the parties. Gallup has measured voting intentions since the 1945 General Election, and the polls have generally produced credible results – except in 1970 (when polling stopped several days before the election and as a result missed a late swing to the Conservatives) and in 1992 (when the polls underestimated Conservative support throughout the campaign).

Of course, a concern may be that the polls actually influence voting behaviour. Someone who has no clear party alignment may use polling information to determine their own vote. This could have an influence in one of two ways. First, the 'bandwagon effect' implies that a party's leading position is reinforced. Second, the 'underdog effect' means that voters support a non-leading party. However, as both imply that issues are less important than the fickle nature of public opinion, voters are unlikely to admit to either of these (Broughton, 1995, p. 98).

It has been suggested that John Major used the information from opinion polls to set the date for the 1992 election (Butler and Kavanagh, 1992, p. 135). A total of fifty polls were conducted in the month before the 1992 General Election which forecast both Conservative and Labour Party victories (Smith, 1996, p. 535), and the polls accounted for approximately one-fifth of the total election coverage in 1992. Of the four polls published on election day, only one put the Conservatives slightly ahead. This was Gallup, which was still seven points adrift of the actual level of Conservative support. Much analysis has taken place since 1992 in an attempt to explain why the polls were wrong, and the Market Research Society commissioned its own investigation. The initially plausible explanations identified were; poor sampling, respondents lying; a late swing; and differential response rates. Which, if any, of these, proved to be correct? The Market Research Society Report, published in 1994, concluded that the following explanations were primarily responsible for the incorrect claims:

1   *Sample bias* Initially it was suggested that sampling may have been skewed – it may be that some who said they would vote Labour were actually not registered due to the effects of the Poll Tax (see McLean and Smith, 1995). Yet broader concerns focused upon the accuracy of the whole process of quota sampling. Quota sampling in 1992 was based upon information from the National Readership Survey (the 1991 census would have been extremely useful, but the data were not available), and 'quotas and weights did not reflect sufficiently accurately the social profile of the

electorate . . . it transpired that these weights were inaccurate relative to those of the census, and again the biases all seemed to favour Labour' (Smith, 1996, pp. 537–541). Therefore, the problem was not using quota sampling as a whole, but the way in which the quotas were implemented in 1992. For example, quota targets for voters living in council housing ranged between 17.5 per cent and 26 per cent, whilst the National Readership Survey under-represented those in the managerial and professional classes (Broughton, 1995, p. 56). Hence, the quotas included too few middle-class voters and too many Labour supporters.

2   *Differential response rate and differential non-response rate*   In 1992, Conservative voters were less willing to admit their allegiance than Labour or Liberal Democrat supporters. Conservative voters were more likely to give an incorrect response to the intention to vote question, or merely refused to take part in the poll. A total of 10 per cent of those polled in 1992 were refusers, which was higher than normal, and evidence from re-polling after the election shows that those who did not express a choice tended to vote Conservative. This phenomenon has become known as the 'Spiral of Silence', after work carried out by Elizabeth Noelle-Neuman. During the 1992 election campaign, the Labour Party scored well on 'soft issues' such as health and education, while the Conservatives scored well on issues such as the quality of the leader, taxation policy and competency in running the economy (Moon, 1999, p. 130). Respondents may have decided to portray a caring voting choice rather than a self-interested choice when confronted by the pollsters.

3   *Late swing*   Neil Kinnock in particular blamed the anti-Labour press for a late swing. However if inaccuracies are caused by this, there is little that can be done to avoid it as opinion polls are only accurate at the time they are taken. The Market Research Society found that there was a small amount of late swing, although this does not overcome the problem that the 1992 polls were consistently incorrect and as such a 'late swing' was not wholly responsible for their mistakes.

Other explanations have also been identified:

1   *Wording important*   The substance of the polls themselves may have created inaccuracies. For example, different responses are elicited depending on whether the question asks about health or the NHS or about jobs instead of unemployment. It is widely recognised that the state of the economy is an important issue in voting choice, but opinion polls use very different questions to analyse this. For example, NOP found that three-quarters said they would pay more tax to fund better public services, but a majority said they trusted or preferred the Conservatives to manage the economy. As such, 'questions on taxation versus public spending have been only weakly correlated with voting choice' (Butler and Kavanagh, 1992, p. 147).

Did any of the other explanations prove to be incorrect? There is no evidence that those polled deliberately lied (Broughton, 1995, p. 94) or that the votes of expatriates (living abroad and entitled to vote but who could not be surveyed by the polls) led to an unexpected Conservative victory (Moon, 1999, p. 116).

So what happened in 1997? The number of opinion polls carried out during the campaign declined slightly compared to 1992. All the polls predicted a Labour Party victory, although considering the actual result and the overwhelming Labour landslide the pollsters would have been in considerable trouble had they been wrong about the overall winner! The quotas for sampling were drawn from large-scale government surveys such as the General Household Survey (Moon, 1999, p. 185). Curtice (1997, p. 451) points out that there was still 'substantial variation' between the Labour Party lead as reported by the different polling companies, and this derived from the methodological revisions that had been implemented after 1992. In fact, the Labour lead ranged from ten points (ICM) to twenty-two points (NOP) when the actual lead was 12.9 per cent (Crewe, 1997, p. 69). Curtice cites evidence from 1997 that question wording may have been influential. ICM, for example, asked voters about voting intention and named the party alternatives. This appeared to increase the level of support for the Liberal Democrats compared to the same question which did not name the parties (Curtice, 1997, p. 454). The polling firms ICM and Gallup both switched to using telephone polling using random-digit dialling (Crewe, 1997, p. 64). Telephone interviews (94 per cent of the population owned telephones) using quasi-random sampling appeared to produce the most accurate results, and Curtice (1997, p. 452) concludes that quota sampling was 'just as ineffective in acquiring representative samples as it had been five years previously'. Therefore, the pollsters may not have developed a foolproof tool for measuring voting intentions at election time, particularly as 1997 saw a rise in non-uniform constituency behaviour.

Conclusion

We have shown in this chapter that surveys and questionnaires are a potentially powerful method of data collection in our search for an understanding of political attitudes and behaviour. The lessons which have been, and are still being, learnt from earlier studies have promoted survey analysis to an almost 'science-like' status. Indeed, although surveys may appear to offer a relatively quick and cheap research tool, the actual process of survey design can be time-consuming and expensive, and it is vital that we get this right if our survey outcomes are to be of any real value.

The opinion polling industry provides us with a valuable insight into the strengths and limitations of survey research, particularly in relation to the dynamics of public opinion and the extent to which people are prepared willingly to reveal personal information. Of course, the main concern in terms of political research is the extent to which the 'general public' is interested in, or understands, the issues we are researching. As Broughton (1995, pp. 44–45) points out:

> The main criticism of some attitudinal questions is that they are trying to be too up-to-date, asking respondents to give answers on topics about which they know little even if the topics have been discussed in the media recently.

Opinion polls continue to play a crucial role for the parties and the media at election time and, despite the events of 1992, Moon argues that pollsters have a good track record which justifies the existence of survey research.

Further reading

For guidance on choosing survey samples and the advantages and disadvantages of the different sampling procedures, see R.A. Bernstein and J.A. Dyer, *An Introduction to Social Science Methods*, 3rd edn, Englewood Cliffs, NJ: Prentice-Hall, 1992, ch. 3.

For guidance on constructing a survey, particularly in relation to valid questions, see Bernstein and Dyer, ibid., ch. 6; and J.B. Mannheim and R.C. Rich, *Empirical Political Analysis*, 4th edn, New York: Longman, 1995, chs 7 and 8.

For a guide to using scaling techniques for constructing survey questions, see Mannheim and Rich, ibid., ch. 9.

For a detailed analysis of opinion polling, I recommend D. Broughton, *Public Opinion Polling and Politics in Britain*, Hemel Hempstead: Harvester Wheatsheaf, 1995; or N. Moon, *Opinion Polls: History, Theory and Practice*, Manchester: Manchester University Press, 1999, which is a little more advanced and looks at the issue from the pollsters' perspective.

Chapter 4

Analysing official data for political research

Introduction: what are 'official statistics'?

Not all the data we use as political scientists are self-generated. In Chapter 3 we discussed the use of surveys and recommended that replicating existing stringently tested questions is one means of establishing good research. Yet we may also choose (or need) to conduct secondary analyses; that is, we make use of data which have been gathered and published by others (rather than construct our own survey on party preference we may, for example, simply choose to make use of the results of opinion polls). In this chapter we shall consider established sources of data, in the form of official statistics, and some of the advantages and disadvantages associated with them. Established sources of data collection are crucial for contemporary research, partly because of their volume and depth. Indeed, Slattery (1986, p. 4) defines official statistics as 'the very lifeblood of modern bureaucracy'. Official statistics cover themes such as the economy, the labour market, welfare, and populations and migration. Briefing box 4.1 lists some of the most predominant sources. First, though, it is necessary to identify some key sources, identify how they are collected, and identify what sort of data they provide.

The Registrar General's Office formalises the registering of births, deaths and marriages. The Family Expenditure Survey (FES) aids the construction of the Retail Price Index, which helps to establish the cost of living and is used to estimate levels of poverty. The Labour Force Survey (LFS) aids European Union (EU) policy making and regional development; indeed, conducting the LFS is compulsory for EU member states. Originally a biannual survey, the LFS has been conducted quarterly since 1992 (Owen, 1999, p. 22), and it covers 60,000 households (approximately 150,000 people; Denman, 1994, p. 6). The General Household Survey (GHS) and British Social Attitudes Survey (BSAS) both measure changes in social attitudes. Other forms of official data are provided by the Office for National Statistics, established in the 1990s as a merger of the Office of Population Censuses and Surveys (OPCS) and the Central Statistical Office.

Briefing box 4.1 Sources of official data

1801	10-yearly Census began
1837	The Registrar General's Office established
1941	The Central Statistical Office established
1957	The Family Expenditure Survey established
1970	The Office of Population Censuses and Surveys established
1973	The General Household Survey established
1979	The Labour Force Survey established
1982	The British Crime Survey established
1983	The British Social Attitudes Survey ('Social Trends') established
1993	The Family Resources Survey established
1996	The Office for National Statistics established

All these surveys are examples of continual data collection, regularly repeated in order to map out changes and trends. Yet we can also identify examples of one-off surveys, such as the 1984 Women and Employment Survey. International sources of secondary data also exist, for example, *Eurostat* (statistics covering EU member states). The Organisation for Economic Co-operation and Development (OECD) is an international organisation which compares data on health and unemployment.

Official statistics are collected in two ways. First, via *statutory requirement* (official registers or forms), as exemplified by the Census. Second, by *voluntary methods*: surveys such as the British Social Attitudes studies (Slattery, 1986, p. 9). The British Social Attitudes surveys are carried out annually by the National Centre for Social Research (NCSR) in order to identify 'underlying changes in people's attitudes and values', and the NCSR also participates in the International Social Survey Programme, a cross-national survey of thirty-three nations (Jowell *et al.*, 1999, pp. xi–xiv).

Despite the fact that we know that each individual person is different, as political scientists we often rely upon aggregate levels of data – why? Aggregate data help us in our quest to identify trends and make predictions. Therefore, aggregate figures are 'obtained by averaging over very many people: individual idiosyncrasies tend to be smoothed out in the process' (Fielding and Gilbert, 2000, p. 12). Therefore, aggregate data help us to appreciate general trends, which can be very useful for comparative analysis (such as levels of voter turnout across countries) but, at the same time, they 'cover up' unusual cases. This can lead to a problem of *ecological fallacy* – where we identify statistical relationships at the aggregate level which in fact do not accurately reflect the corresponding relationship at the individual data level (Miller, 1995, p. 155). Furthermore, and of particular importance when trying to understand official statistics, our inability to scrutinise the raw data means that aggregate data can hide biases, because it is not apparent exactly *how* the trends have been calculated.

Official statistics are particularly important for our understanding of *demographics* – that is, patterns of stability and change in the study of human populations. For example, to ensure that housing provisions are adequate, we need to understand how particular regions are affected by migration patterns. As we are living in a society where life expectancy is gradually increasing, this may have implications for the *type* of housing which is required. If a new company wishes to locate in an area with a good resource of labour, it may be useful to have some awareness of levels of unemployment, the gender balance and the age distribution among the local population.

Access to official statistics (which we shall discuss in more detail below) varies: some data are available free of charge, whereas other data have costs. Blakemore contrasts the availability of UK data with that of other countries: the USA has no direct data charges, whilst in North Korea there is considerable secrecy surrounding official statistics (Blakemore, 1999, p. 47). Therefore, there are plenty of 'official' data collected: How might we utilise it in political research?

Are official statistics neutral measures?

The Office for National Statistics (ONS) produces a vast wealth of data, most of which receives very little publicity and attracts minimal public interest. Some sorts of data, however, become the focus of political and media scrutiny – in particular, crime figures, hospital waiting lists and unemployment statistics (Owen, 1999, p. 19). As was discussed in relation to surveys in Chapter 3, data produced for official purposes often need to ensure confidentiality and anonymity of those surveyed, and therefore we should not be surprised that a potential tension exists between the individual's and the public's rights and interests. As a direct result, the limitations on the public scrutiny of official data 'removes the power of challenge'. A 1996 ONS press release stated that the organisation aimed to increase accessibility whilst maintaining confidentiality, and the basic rule is that statistics created for administrative purposes are the most restricted (Dale, 1999, pp. 29–31).

The Government Statisticians' Collective (GSC) (1993) suggests that government secrecy ensures that there is little public awareness of the process of official statistics collection. In fact, controversy over the collection process and interpretation of official data is exacerbated by the fact that the 'target audience' is administrators, civil servants and ministers and, to a lesser extent, industry and commerce. Indeed, the interests and concerns of academic researchers have a low priority (p. 146); see also Blakemore, 1999, p. 48). Slattery (1986) identifies several questions which need to be asked when using established sources of data (see Briefing box 4.2).

Perrons (1999, p. 105) suggests that official statistics often, perhaps unintentionally, have been undermined by a gender bias due to the fact that they concentrate upon the 'public sphere' such as paid work and particular crimes. For example, *'official crime'* is measured by two sources: police reports and the British Crime Survey (BCS), and crime statistics are published annually. The BCS is effectively a 'household victimisation survey' (Povey, 1995, p. 9) and is important because not all crimes are reported to the police. There are some offences not included in the Home Office's 'notifiable offences' category (most motoring offences, prostitution), whilst the BCS only covers offences against individuals and their property but excludes commercial crime. Therefore, although there may be considerable overlap, the two data sources present separate pictures. In other words, the aggregate data presented by both

---

Briefing box 4.2 Underlying concerns surrounding official data

- Who has sponsored the research?
- How have the findings been interpreted?
- How are concepts defined?
- Why are particular social and political issues prioritised over others?
- What are the results going to be used for?
- Who was studied?

Source: Slattery (1986)

---

sources are often different, not because one source is incorrect, but because different cases are used as the basis for calculation. A problem, then, with the official crime statistics is that offences such as domestic violence may generally be under-reported (Perrons, 1999, p. 112), whilst what becomes a criminal fact is often determined by organisational practices and power relations (May, 1997, pp. 69–71).

Traditionally, statistical information was generated by the government with the intention of operationalising comparative analyses of social development and change. However, this has been undermined by the changing 'mode, regularity and timing of publications' (Tant, 1995, p. 255; see the examples outlined below). Tant's underlying concern is not only that data are being manipulated for political gains, but that this is, after all, public information which is increasingly being governed by 'political subjectivity' and increasingly being kept hidden, thus reinforcing the secretive nature of British government (ibid., pp. 264–266; see also Government Statisticians' Collective, 1993, p. 161). Even when official statistics are published, their implications can be hidden or overlooked. For example, the Black Report on health inequalities (which made use of GHS data) was given a limited circulation, particularly among journalists; and the 1986 Health and Personal Social Services Statistics for England were published the day before a royal wedding – tactics which Tant (1995, pp. 256–257) refers to as 'bad news diversion'.

In order to appreciate the 'political' nature of official data, May (1997, pp. 74–75) identifies three schools of thought which take different approaches to the usefulness of these statistics:

1   *the realist school* upholds the belief that official statistics are objective indicators of what they are measuring;
2   *the institutionalist school* rejects the notion that official statistics can be valid or reliable. Thus they cannot be objective, but do tell us something about the emphasis of priorities within group interests;
3   *the radical school* agrees with institutionalists that official statistics represent and organise priorities; however, they believe that these priorities are located within a wider theory of the dynamics and structure of society. For example, those belonging to the radical school believe that statistics are produced on health and income in order to regulate the population. Therefore, because official statistics can be manipulated: 'The realist will look for more accurate techniques for generating such information; the radical will criticize and use such information as indicative of more immediate or wider power inequalities in society and the institutionalist will concentrate on the process of their production' (May, 1997, p. 79).

Unsurprisingly, governments have frequently been accused of 'massaging' official statistics; that is, manipulating figures 'in order to create desired impressions' (Government Statisticians' Collective, 1993, p. 162). The very nature of aggregate data enables the producers to 'alter' the remit of what is being counted to present what is often a more favourable short-term picture. The GSC identifies four types of massage:

1   *Changing the definition of terms*   See the example of 'unemployment' below.

2   *The 'unjustifiable extrapolation of trends'* By manipulating the parameters of the time periods studied, governments can ensure that data are as favourable as possible. When, for example, government figures indicate the 'yearly trend', does that mean the calendar year? Often not – it could be the twelve months prior to some economic or political crisis. If a short period (such as three months) is used to predict an annual trend, the selection of those particular three months can produce very different results.

3   *The manipulation of adjustments by turning data from raw to adjusted figures* That is, taking into account some form of context; for example, 'seasonally adjusted' unemployment figures. This is a good example of the way in which aggregate data can obscure what is really occurring at the individual level.

4   *The manipulation of categories* For example, making age groups smaller or larger; putting certain figures into a general category entitled 'other' or 'miscellaneous'.

Therefore, we can see that official statistics are not neutral figures: their content and availability is often revised for what, intentionally or unintentionally, may seem to be political ends. Official statistics serve primarily an administrative purpose, and as Dorling and Simpson (1999, p. 4) point out, unemployment statistics do not measure the number of people who want jobs, health statistics do not measure health or care needs, and housing statistics do not measure homelessness or housing needs. What they do actually measure will be considered in a later section of this chapter, when we shall examine the ways in which official statistics have been 'manipulated' – often to the benefit of the government's interests.

The development and collection of official data

Official statistics have been generated by governments for centuries. Early examples of official statistics were used to enable the effective collection of taxes and to find suitable candidates for conscription (Slattery, 1986, p. 19). In the eleventh century, the Domesday Book provided the first national social survey of England (Dorling and Simpson, 1999, p. 2). Concerns about poverty motivated Edwin Chadwick's (1842) *Report on the Sanitary Conditions of the Labouring Population in Great Britain* and Booth's 1899 study of London (Lee, 1999, p. 173). A contemporary counterpart of the Domesday Book is the Census which is carried out only at ten-yearly intervals (it is such a lengthy process that a shorter time span would not be practical). Completing the Census has been compulsory in Britain since 1920 and it is recognised as the only comprehensive source of information on immigration and what is classed as the 'working' population (Slattery, 1986, p. 27). Initially, the Census was seen as purely a population count, but since 1841 the information on individuals has become more detailed. The information provides data on a very local level, assists resource allocation by central and local government, and aids town and country planning (Diamond, 1999, pp. 9–10).

Levitas and Guy (1996, p. 2) suggest that two particular developments have had a significant impact in the collection of official statistics. Between 1967 and 1978, the quality and scope of the data collected was expanded, whilst after 1981, the scope of social statistics was cut. This has been compounded by the fact that the cost of government publications has significantly increased, which has served to limit general access to what many see as public data (Levitas, 1996, p. 12). It comes as no surprise, then, that academic assessment of the validity of official statistics in the post-war period has become increasingly sceptical.

An obvious concern a researcher has to face when employing official statistics is the extent to which they are reliable and valid – issues we have already discussed in Chapter 2. This means that we need to categorise the same acts or situations in exactly the same way, categories must be mutually exclusive and must be exhaustive (discussed in Chapter 2 in relation to using SPSS). To recap, by 'exclusive' we mean that a person cannot fall into two age groups. By 'exhaustive' we recognise the full range of possible age groups (presuming that we are not focusing upon particular age groups only). In real-life political analysis, very careful consideration needs to be given to these two qualities. We may for convenience use the label 'retired' when classifying occupational status, but at the aggregate level this will hide a much more useful level of information (and therefore classification by previous occupation may be more useful). Official statistics have been somewhat undermined in status, as governments have on numerous occasions been accused of manipulating them for political gain. Tant (1995) argues that official statistics are used to initiate policy, define 'social problems' and justify new social policies to resolve these social problems. For example, the Conservative government (1979–97) blamed the existence of poverty upon individual deficits rather than the socio-economic system. More blatantly during this period of government, the method used to compile the Unemployment Register was altered more than thirty times, with most changes leading to a decrease in the number of people 'officially' unemployed. So what alterations can we identify?

Changes in official data collection

In this section we shall focus upon examples of deliberate changes and potential flaws in the definition of concepts measured by official statistics.

Classless society?

For official purposes, the Registrar General's classification system is used to define social class by occupation. At the time of the 1851 Census, a predominantly industrial system of classification was introduced (Nichols, 1996, p. 68). The commonly accepted scale today is outlined in Briefing box 4.3.

As a result of a post-war shift from traditional manual to non-manual types of employment, British society has apparently become more middle class. How reliable is this? How do we decide which jobs fit into which class category? This problem is demonstrated by the fact that Cabinet ministers promoted themselves from group II to group I in 1981 (Slattery, 1986, p. 48). Nichols (1996, p. 71) reveals that in the 1951 Classification of Occupations the titles 'capitalist', 'landowner', 'expert' and 'lunatic' were all placed in the 'missing' category! A grey area generally exists

Briefing box 4.3 Registrar General's social classification scale

I	Professional
II	Intermediate
IIIa	Skilled non-manual
IIIb	Skilled manual
IV	Semi-skilled manual
V	Unskilled manual

Source: Slattery (1986, p. 48)

between which occupations are labelled as skilled manual labour and which are lower middle class.

Also, many 'occupational' scenarios are ignored or underestimated by the Registrar General's classification. These include: 'work' carried out in the home; the self-employed; the unemployed; and the retired (the latter two being either left out or classified by the last occupation held; Slattery, 1986, p. 50). Despite the fact that the Registrar General's definitions are revised (if necessary) every 10 years, there are limitations in using occupation alone as a measure of class. Social stratification is also decided by gender, race and power. As we mentioned earlier, official statistics may be gender-biased and Perrons (1999, p. 105) points to the need to restructure employment categories to take account of the 'universal feminisation of employment', particularly in the service sector. Thus, the *official* method of measuring social class heavily focuses upon status (Nichols, 1996, p. 67), demonstrating the 'acceptance of a hierarchical social structure, of brain being superior to brawn and of social mobility being a truly open avenue for the rise of the talented, ambitious, and hard working' (Slattery, 1986, p. 51).

To work or not to work, that is the definition . . .

Unemployment is perhaps one of the most 'political' concepts in official statistics because it fundamentally affects the cost of the welfare state and can ultimately affect the result of elections. Slattery (1986, p. 89) argues that the official definition of unemployed 'is primarily an administrative one that attempts to keep both the size and cost of the problem to a minimum', and the emphasis changed in 1982 from a registrant-based count to a claimant-based count (Levitas, 1996a, p. 48). What is the difference? Two statistical series are utilised to measure unemployment in the UK: the Labour Force Survey (LFS) series counts the number of people seeking work, while the monthly claimant count enumerates the number of people entitled to unemployment benefit. Each identifies different, but overlapping, sectors of the unemployed population: the claimant count favours men, the LFS women, whilst there are more older and younger people registered as unemployed under the LFS than under the claimant count (Denman, 1994, p. 6). Not only have definitions been redefined, but we should also appreciate that unemployment is not a consistent feature; for example, the proportion of long-term unemployed increases with age, unemployment affects manual workers as a group the hardest, and there are significant regional trends to unemployment. Problems of exact statistics are also confounded by what jobs are available and their suitability: there is a notable difference between unemployment and underemployment and the stability of employment.

If we were to rely solely upon the administrative claimant count to define unemployment, then the official data would exclude a massive number of non-registered and 'hidden' people, merely because they do not claim unemployment benefit (see Briefing box 4.4).

We can identify explicit cases where the *official* unemployment definition was changed, and these changes were to the government's benefit. In 1982, Norman Tebbit (then Employment Minister) changed the rules to exclude those not claiming unemployment benefit, which cut the figure of *officially* unemployed by 246,000. In 1983, men over 60 on higher long-term rates of supplementary benefit were excluded, cutting the *officially* unemployed figure by 162,000 (Slattery, 1986, p. 83). The rules were again changed in 1986 so that *official* claimants had to declare themselves available to work in the next 24 hours – a rule which adversely affects women with children; and in 1988, the Social Security Act removed entitlement for almost all under-18 year olds (Levitas, 1996a, p. 49). Over time, those who were once unemployed have been transferred to other forms of classification, for example, those in receipt of incapacity benefit or the long-term sick, in order to narrow further the definition of *officially* unemployed (Thomas, 1999, p. 325).

The progressive and numerous changes in the definition of *officially unemployed* people have rendered the claimant count statistics a 'virtually useless indicator' for comparative purposes, whilst certain groups, such as women and the young, are affected in more ways than others by the changing definitions (Levitas, 1996a, pp. 46–47). The inevitable impact of tying official unemployment to eligibility for benefits, and by further reducing the number of those who are eligible for benefits,

---

Briefing box 4.4 Examples of the deregistered or 'unofficial' unemployed

- Temporarily laid-off workers;
- part-time workers;
- the severely sick and disabled;
- students;
- pensioners;
- housewives;
- the long-term unemployed (1+ year).

Source: Slattery (1986, p. 82)

means that the official measure is only a limited picture of what could be classed as unemployed, for example, not in work but wanting to be so (ibid., p. 48).

We have also identified a second source of unemployment data: the LFS, which is carried out quarterly by the ONS, although it is prone to survey-type errors of sampling and response (see Chapter 2). The LFS definition of unemployment differs from the claimant count definition in three respects:

1   all respondents who work at least one hour a week are classed as 'employed' (even though they may still be entitled to benefits);
2   those deemed 'unemployed' must have been seeking work for the last four weeks; this excludes 'discouraged workers';
3   the survey covers the whole population of working age, i.e claimants and non-claimants (Thomas, 1999, p. 329).

The LFS utilises criteria which are broadly similar to those employed by the International Labour Organisation (ILO) and this factor gives the data some comparative value. Denman claimed in 1994 that the two data sources 'currently reinforce one another by showing unemployment standing at approximately the same level, and following a broadly similar trend over time' (p. 4). In comparison, by 1996, the *Guardian* editorial pointed out that the British government's definition of unemployed (that is, not working and claiming benefits) was 222,000 lower than the ILO's definition (those looking for work). The official justification for not changing the method of measurement was that it would cost £8 million (*Guardian*, 22 October 1996).

Waiting around . . .

Official statistics on the population's health really covers the usage of the National Health Service (NHS), as relatively little data on private health care exist (Macfarlane and Head, 1999, p. 223). Information is collected from a range of sources, including statutory notifications (on births, deaths and communicable diseases), claims for National Insurance and Social Security benefits, waiting list returns and the General Household Survey (GHS). Yet this only presents a partial picture as:

> All these data are collected through people's contact with health and social services. This means that people are counted only if a service exists and people are aware of it, want to use it and succeed in doing so.
> (Macfarlane and Head, 1999, p. 227)

We have already alluded to the contentious nature of official waiting list data. A 'waiting list' is defined in terms of the length of time a patient waits for treatment. In order to get on to such a list, a patient first has to see a consultant, which can also involve a considerable wait. As such, the *official* statistics do not consider 'time spent waiting to get on the waiting list' (Tant, 1995, p. 261). Added to this is the fact that waiting lists are constantly being 'tidied up' as people are removed from lists – not because of successful treatment, but because of self-deferral and even death (Macfarlane and Head, 1999, p. 232). We have already mentioned that the Conservative government attempted to hide the findings of the 1980 Black Report which linked ill health to social inequality. Guy (1996, p. 92) points out that, throughout the 1980s and 1990s, the government sought to cover up data on mortality and replace it with 'new statistics' on health which 'represented a new and aggressive, publicity-conscious use of statistics for political purposes'.

Unequal, not poor

Official data on low incomes and poverty have always been controversial (Townsend, 1996, p. 26) and social scientists have had to rely upon data from other sources, particularly after the abolition of the Royal Commission on Income and Wealth in 1979 (Levitas, 1996a, p. 16). The Census is of limited use because it does not ask questions about income or wealth (Lee, 1999, p. 172). Historically, different measures have been used, such as Poor Law statistics from the nineteenth century until 1939 (Southall, 1999, pp. 350–351). In 1989, John Moore (then Secretary of State for Social Services) chose to replace government recognition of poverty with the term *inequality* (Townsend, 1996, p. 27). Despite the fact that data on poverty are collected by a range of bodies, both national (the Child Poverty Action Group, the Low Pay Unit) and international (the United Nations, the World Bank, the ILO), there is a distinct problem in terms of the criteria used to define poverty. Common units of measurement include:

- subsistence income;
- level of basic needs in a community (related to the idea of 'social exclusion');
- resources required to escape 'relative deprivation' (Townsend, 1996, p. 28).

As Owen (1999, p. 24) highlights, 'terms such as "family", "labour" and "resources" have to be understood in their contexts'.

Similar problems exist around the official data on homelessness, not least because there is no universally accepted definition:

> In particular, given the moral and/or statutory duty incumbent upon central and local government to tackle homelessness, it is not surprising that they adopt a fairly strict definition in order to minimise the problem with which they have to deal. Voluntary organisations, on the other hand, without the ultimate responsibility for housing homeless households, can afford to make a more generous assessment of the circumstances in which someone is deemed homeless.
>
> (Widdowfield, 1999, p. 182)

Therefore, here we have a clear example of how official definitions have focused upon a particular sector or area of need. By classifying those who are *officially* homeless as those who successfully apply under the local authority homeless rule, another group who do not apply, do not successfully apply and who live in unsatisfactory accommodation are not officially recognised (ibid., p. 184).

Advantages and disadvantages in using official statistics as a research tool

We cannot escape the fact that valuable data for political research are becoming increasingly dominated by government and its agencies. Slattery (1986, p. 29) outlines the main advantages and disadvantages of official statistics (see Briefing box 4.5).

Therefore, we can see that the sorts of changes we have identified can have important implications for those who wish to research changing trends, but we can also identify broader implications of the political manipulation of official data.

Briefing box 4.5 Advantages and disadvantages of research employing official statistics

Advantages

- Produces a wealth of information relating to political, social and economic issues;
- allows the examination of trends over time;
- may be the only source of information for some issues.

Disadvantages

- Prioritises particular interests and thus sets an agenda;
- the definition of some concepts will change over time: such concepts are *diachronic* (see May, 1997, p. 69);
- the time taken to publish large sections of data may render such statistics out of date;
- is all information published? do governments and agencies withhold information to avoid embarrassment?
- data are quantitative, and as such tell us *what* rather than *why*. The data alone have little value unless we can relate them to theoretical understandings and expectations;
- the response rate to surveys; for example, the 1995 GHS had a 82 per cent response rate, although only 71 per cent of the data sets provided a complete set of data for all household members (Owen, 1999, p. 23).

Public confidence in official statistics

In this last section we shall consider the increasing concern about the validity of official statistics. Public confidence can be undermined in two ways: concerns about the methods of data collection, and concerns about the massaging of figures. Even the Census is not without its problems. In relation to the 1981 Census, only 6000 of the 18 million homes failed to complete the required form (Slattery, 1986,

p. 27). In comparison, the 1991 Census had approximately 2 million people missing, possibly because the Community Charge (or Poll Tax) was in place. Those missing tended to be 18–30 year old males and the very old (Diamond, 1999, p. 17). Of course, the homeless are not represented at all (Townsend, 1996, p. 38). Public concerns about Census data have also emerged in Germany and the Netherlands (Dale, 1999, p. 35).

However, the number of potentially eligible voters who fail to enrol on the electoral register is much higher. The percentage of those who are eligible and who actually enrol has declined from 97.1 per cent in 1976 to 96 per cent in 1990 – a failure to register which is again associated with the Poll Tax (McLean and Smith, 1995, p. 130). This apparent 'concern' that government-collected data may be used to track down Poll Tax evaders is supported by survey data. In January 1991, a Gallup survey carried out three months before the Census asked: '*How confident are you that the Census Office will not reveal an individual's census information to other government departments?*' Only 15 per cent of respondents were 'very confident' that Census data were not passed on, whilst 30 per cent were 'somewhat confident'. More worrying for those attempting to collect accurate information is that some 40 per cent were 'not at all confident' that Census data were not used for other purposes, whilst 15 per cent replied 'don't know' (ibid., p. 145). It is hardly surprising then that the Royal Statistical Society's 1991 Report criticised the Geographical Statistical Service (GSS) for lacking autonomy, for methodological biases and for lack of resources (Levitas, 1996a, p. 22).

Since 1997, the Social Survey Division of the ONS has attempted to monitor public confidence in official statistics. This research shows that, not only do some people have difficulty in distinguishing official data from other forms of statistics (such as opinion polls), but that a large percentage feel that official data are 'misleading'. This misleading quality may be down to governments only publishing positive data (rather than employing dubious methods or lying), although respondents were more sceptical about unemployment data than about cost of living data (a less politically sensitive issue; Goddard, 1999). As the Government Statisticians' Collective (1993, p. 155) points out, the 'problem' with official statistics is that:

> what such statistics tend to monitor is not so much the social conditions of wealth, unemployment or homelessness, but rather the operations of the state agencies responsible for dealing with the matter . . . The consequence, often very convenient to the state, is a lack of reliable information on social problems about which little or nothing is being done.

Conclusion

The main 'weakness' with official statistics is that they vary in terms of their accuracy and the manner in which they are compiled, and as such: 'Official statistics, like social research itself, may employ unexamined assumptions about social life which, if one is not cautious, may be inherited and reproduced in studies' (May, 1997, p. 65).

Tant (1995) claims that official data on social class, health and mortality are becoming increasingly difficult to locate. It may seem a rather cynical evaluation, but we cannot ignore the fact that official statistics are not as objective as we might like to think they should be. This is not particularly aided by the fact that, when the methods of measurement change, they generally seem to work in the government's favour, leading Tant (p. 260) to suggest that 'rather than government being led by the facts, the "facts" seem to be led by government'. Therefore, we need to pay close attention to definitions used within official statistics and we must be critical of why particular information is produced. Who produces official statistics and for what purpose?

Townsend (1996, p. 40) recommends that one solution to the problem would be an independent National Statistical Commission. Indeed, whilst in opposition, the Labour Party put forward proposals for an Independent National Statistical Service (ibid.). As Dale (1999, p. 35) highlights, the ONS relies upon public co-operation and as a result trust in the method of collection, dissemination and overall use is imperative, otherwise high-quality data will not be collected.

Perhaps, as political scientists, we would do well to bear in mind the following set of questions, not only in relation to official statistics, but when we are dealing with any form of quantitative secondary data: 'Is that true? How do I know it is true? Where did it come from? Who wanted me to know that? What are the alternative explanations? Could I have done better?' (Dorling and Simpson, 1999, p. 419).

Certainly, the latter question is one that can be applied as we move from undergraduate to postgraduate studies.

Further reading

A good introduction to official statistics is provided in T. May, *Social Research: Issues, Methods and Process*, 2nd edn, Buckingham: Open University Press, 1997, ch. 4. A more detailed analysis can be located in R. Levitas and W. Guy (eds), *Interpreting Official Statistics*, London: Routledge, 1996; whilst D. Dorling and S. Simpson (eds), *Statistics in Society: The Arithmetic of Politics*, London: Arnold, 1999, provides a wide collection of succinct chapters which deal with the political nature of official statistics.

Part II

QUALITATIVE RESEARCH

Chapter 5

Introducing qualitative analysis

Introduction

In Part II, we move on to consider the advantages and disadvantages of an alternative type of data to that examined in Part I. Here, we consider the role that qualitative data can play in political research, along with the various advantages and disadvantages of adopting such an approach. Qualitative data can be analysed in various formats, and within the next four chapters we shall consider the opportunities offered by the research formats of observational research (including participant observation), interviews, documents and media resources. We begin in this chapter by contrasting the recognised differences between quantitative and qualitative research, and consider the development of the ethnographic research approach. We shall focus upon the general strengths and weaknesses of qualitative research and consider the circumstances in which it can be used in political research, by considering some existing case studies. As we shall consider interviews in greater detail in Chapter 6, we only consider some general principles relevant to this research tool here, and we focus in greater detail in this chapter upon observational research.

What is the difference between quantitative and qualitative research? Do they produce different results?

In the previous chapters we demonstrated that quantitative research focuses upon the analysis of numerical data, and in doing so usually makes use of large sets of data to make generalisations and predictions. In comparison, qualitative research analyses political behaviour and attitudes which it is not possible or desirable to quantify. Put another way, qualitative research 'tends to focus on exploring, in as much detail as possible, smaller numbers of instances or examples which are seen as being interesting or illuminating, and aims to achieve "depth" rather than "breadth"' (Blaxter *et al.*, 1996, p. 60). It is generally accepted, therefore, that qualitative research allows for greater expression and insight. However, that is not to say that the two forms of data collection are mutually exclusive – a research question is often answerable from both approaches; it is just that we analyse the evidence in different ways. Indeed, research projects often adopt both approaches: either to ensure validity in the findings or to offer different interpretations of the same phenomenon because different concerns are prioritised. Just as quantitative research can employ primary and secondary data sources, the same rule applies to qualitative research (particularly if existing documentary or interview material is made available).

The origins of qualitative research methods lie in anthropology and sociology. Qualitative research began to flourish in the nineteenth century – Engels' research into *The Conditions of the Working Class in England* is a classic example. Devine (1995, p. 137) claims that the positive gains of a qualitative approach within political science are often neglected, when indeed its strengths lie in the fact that it 'involves the researcher immersing her/himself in the social setting in which s/he is interested, observing people in their usual milieux and participating in their activities'. We can see from Devine's comments that the process of qualitative research is not a 'detached' form of research in the same way, say, as large-scale surveys, where we experience little if any personal contact with those being studied. We can quite happily ask complete strangers to fill out questionnaires, but we cannot carry out qualitative research in the same way – we need to know, or at least become knowledgeable, about who or what we are researching and we need to do this in the subjects' natural environment, as opposed to an 'experimental' setting (see our reference to the 'problems' of political experiments in Chapter 1).

Relating to our second question – whether the two approaches produce different results – although the methodological tools are different for quantitative and qualitative research, the two approaches are often used in tandem, providing *different types of evidence* to research *the same research question*. Quantitative methods have been espoused by the Positivist School, where there is a strong emphasis upon measuring concepts. Interaction between the researcher and the individual being studied tends to be limited, and there is a notion of describing an external reality. Qualitative interviews, in contrast, are useful because they allow people to talk freely and present their perspective *in their terms*. In comparison to simply ticking boxes on a questionnaire, in-depth interviews allow interviewees to use their own language, so the discussion should flow more freely. Think back to our discussion of surveys in Chapter 3 when we considered the role of closed questions in survey design. Imagine asking respondents the following question:

Q. *Which is your most common form of political activity?*
☐ *voting*
☐ *attending political meetings*
☐ *other*

What if everyone ticks the 'other' category? We would learn two lessons. First, the categories are too narrow (which a pilot study may well have found out). Second, we cannot return to ask what 'other' means and therefore the results are of very limited use. By asking the same question in an interview, we might learn (a) what activity is/is not undertaken, but more importantly (b) what the respondent understands the term political to mean.

An important way in which qualitative and quantitative methods differ is in terms of sampling. We demonstrated in Chapter 2 that snowball sampling is a useful technique and it is certainly more common in qualitative research, where probability sampling is unlikely to be feasible. In contrast to the sampling techniques we would expect of a large-scale survey, with qualitative research 'sampling is often guided by the search for contrasts which are needed to clarify the analysis and achieve maximum identification of emergent categories' (Burns, 2000, p. 289). Therefore, we are looking for '*different examples of*' rather than an accurate sub-population, and by comparing those we are studying we can use cross-referencing to try to eliminate some of the subjectivity.

In Chapter 3, we discussed the growing use of opinion polling within politics, focusing particularly upon the changing techniques and the limitations of this particular quantitative analysis of public opinion. In recognition of the limitations of simple survey data, parties and pollsters also employ qualitative tools – sometimes referred to as 'focus groups'. Focus groups can be employed at various research stages: for formulating a research question; for developing relevant indicators for data collection (that is, distinguishing the important indicators from the unimportant ones); and for producing data to answer the research question itself. In terms of their operationalisation: '*Focus group* methods involve bringing together small groups of carefully selected individuals for an in-depth discussion of some topic; guided by a *moderator*, in order to learn how people think about that topic' (Mannheim and Rich, 1995, p. 370).

Focus groups contain an average of eight to ten interviewees (compared to quantitative surveys which can poll several hundred or even thousands at any particular time). The advantages of focus groups over surveys are:

1   they ensure that the research question is covered;
2   they can overcome the problem of wording that may be encountered with surveys and the possibility of interviewer effects;
3   an explanation of answers can be requested;
4   it is possible to recognise how opinions are given in relation to the answers and reactions of others.

In other words: 'The central feature of focus group methods is that they *rely on interaction among the participants to generate insights into the subject under study*' (ibid., p. 372).

This means that we can, via group discussion, begin to appreciate whether opinions are strongly held or relatively weak, and whether respondents are likely to change their minds on the subject (what we referred to as the 'intensity' of public opinion in Chapter 3). Qualitative polling is used by political parties to test policy proposals – particularly the *wording* of proposals – 'to gain an understanding of how citizens see problems, evaluate services, and are likely to react to new programs' (ibid., p. 370). For example, in-depth interviewing was employed by the Conservative Party in the early 1980s in an attempt to look at the psychology of voters, although the strategy was quickly dropped as it was deemed to be too costly (Broughton, 1995, p. 113). Focus group research has also been employed by the Labour Party to test, for example, ideas which later appeared in the 1989 Labour Party Policy Review (ibid., p. 112). The Labour Party also employed qualitative research in the run-up to the 1992 General Election to test pre-election broadcasts, policy packages and the shadow budget, and during the election itself held qualitative group interviews with floating voters in marginal seats (Butler and Kavanagh, 1992, pp. 150–151). A continuation of this research strategy immediately after the 1992 election demonstrated 'a deep hostility to Labour as old-fashioned and opposed to the ordinary aspirations of an increasingly prosperous electorate' (ibid., 1992, p. 151).

Therefore, while the Labour Party may have pursued the right policy initiatives in 1992, voters demonstrated through qualitative research that they did not necessarily trust them to keep their promises. It is perhaps not unsurprising then that focus groups played a large role in Labour's preparations for the 1997 General Election (associated in particular with the work of Philip Gould).

The ethnographic approach in qualitative research

In contrast to the positivist approach, those who espouse qualitative methods adopt what we refer to as an *ontological* position – acknowledging that reality is not objective. If we relate this to the earlier comment made by Devine – that the researcher needs to be immersed in the social setting of the research focus – we can begin to appreciate that context is the driving force behind qualitative research: what we are really seeking to answer is not only *'what happens'* but *'why'* and *'how'*. It is all very well knowing how many people voted for the Referendum Party in 1997, but it is far more informative to know why they chose to vote this way (it could not, after all, be due to long-term alignment). We may know that membership of political parties is declining, but if the parties wish to reverse the trend, they must understand why people choose/choose not to join. However, as Halfpenny (1984) points out, a researcher may be faced with the problem of communicating findings to an audience with no direct contact with that culture. This was an issue raised by Heclo and Wildavsky (1974) in their study of public spending, as they acknowledged that they were attempting to explain a policy making process which was largely unexplored and unquestioned by the general public (p. xix).

Ethnomethodology is strongly associated with the work of sociologists such as Garfinkel and the Chicago School of Sociology which developed in the USA in the 1920s and 1930s, and is primarily concerned with the way in which people construct and convey meaning:

> Ethnomethodology is founded on the view that every occurrence within the social world is unique or indexical: that is, every event depends for its sense on the context within which it occurs, where the context is made up of the time, the place and the people involved.
>
> (Halfpenny, 1984, p. 8)

For ethnographers, *ethnocentrism* (cultural bias) is avoided by emphasising the centrality of *cultural relativism* (the means by which a society is constructed and operates – the 'rules' of political behaviour). Again, with Heclo and Wildavsky's study, their research approach focused not just on who made spending decisions, but upon the dynamics of the relationship between political actors and political administrators. Political scientists have frequently described the Civil Service as the 'Whitehall Village', implying that the expected processes of behaviour here are different from political behaviour exhibited in other political institutions. Therefore, in order to analyse political opinions and behaviour, we must also be aware of the context in which these opinions are formed and the behaviour takes place:

> Ethnography, then, contrasts with 'scientific' methods of social science research that, based upon a universalistic model of science, emphasize its neutrality and objectivity, attempting to generate data untouched by human hands. Ethnography belongs to the theoretical tradition which argues that the 'facts' of society and culture belong to a different order from those of nature.
>
> (Walsh, 1998, pp. 217–218)

The emphasis within ethnography is upon explanatory understandings rather than upon trying to make predictions about what might occur. It does not make prior assumptions about what is important or what to expect. The influence of the cultural context is central, and the research approach allows for the focus of the research to change during the course of data collection. Therefore, it is an inductive, not a deductive, research approach. Most qualitative research tends to take an inductive methodological approach – that is, the theory develops from empirical observation in which we identify patterns (Marsh and Stoker, 1995). Thus what we develop is *grounded theory* – the theory develops from the research, rather than from us testing an hypothesis (Foster, 1996, pp. 60–61). The principles of grounded theory have developed through the work of Glaser and Strauss since the 1960s, and are based upon the concept of *analytic induction*, although we should be wary of making the assumption that evidence of patterns automatically entitles us to become theory builders. A difference exists between significant patterns (that is, theory-related) and general trends.

All this does not imply that quantitative and qualitative methods of research provide mutually exclusive types of evidence, only that the method of collecting data is different. For example, surveys provide only limited information and are often best for telling us what people do rather than why they do it. As Devine (1994, p. 219) points out, the relationship between political behaviour and political attitudes is a complex one: 'it is highly problematic to presume behaviour is an indicator of attitudes and vice versa'. Just because social class *x* tends to vote for party *y*, this does not mean that the two are directly related. While we may be able to explain in some detail the reasons for taking political action, we may never be at the stage where we can say that a certain characteristic always results in a particular political action. What we shall now do is to focus upon the practical issues surrounding qualitative political research, particularly via the tool of observation.

The advantages and disadvantages of employing qualitative data in political research

We have previously mentioned that in the process of research we can employ two types of data. If we adopt a qualitative approach, we may choose to gather primary data, and we can do this via two particular research tools: interviews and observation. Alternatively (and as supplementary) we can analyse existing data – be it in the form of official documents, reports, biographical studies or the media – and we shall consider these sources of research data in Chapters 7 and 8. In this chapter and in Chapter 6 we shall consider some of the issues relevant to gathering our own data in a qualitative form.

In Chapter 3 we examined the strengths and weaknesses of using attitude scales and surveys in political research. One particular problem with surveys is that politics is often a deeply personal topic, and certain beliefs and issues simply cannot be tapped into by a survey. Might any of these problems be overcome by employing a qualitative approach?

We can see from Briefing box 5.1 that qualitative research tends to have a much more 'personable' quality. That is, we get to know the person/group of people we are

Briefing box 5.1 The strengths and weakness of qualitative research

Strengths

- Greater opportunity to explore beliefs and attitudes;
- can explain 'why' and 'how' rather than just 'what';
- greater reliance upon the respondent's actions and thoughts.

Weaknesses

- Data are atypical: limited, if any, ability to generalise;
- problem of interpretation: different researchers may interpret the same response in different ways;
- researcher involvement: may become involved in, and be sympathetic towards particular participants ('going native');
- time-consuming.

Source: Adapted from Devine (1994)

researching, often to the extent that we learn far more than is necessary for the particular research project. For example, we might become familiar with a person's family and social background, their concerns and their aspirations for the future. In fact, we come to see the political world from *their* perspective. The down side, of course, is that what we learn is just one, unique, experience. Broadly speaking, we cannot make generalisations from our findings. The reasons for one person's political beliefs and thoughts *cannot* be generalised to anybody else (even though we might uncover patterns and trends).

Schofield (1993) claims that the importance of generalisability has been central to developments in quantitative research, yet in the qualitative literature it 'appears to be a widely shared view that it is unimportant, unachievable, or both' (p. 201). We have said in previous chapters that good quantitative research is expected to be representative and reliable; that is, we should be able to repeat our findings in later studies. We hope to be able to make generalisations from quantitative research with a relative degree of certainty. However, it is often the case that qualitative research is neither replicable or comparable. Indeed, those interested in cultural anthropology or who conduct detailed single-case studies are unlikely to be concerned with generalisability. Yet despite the problems of accessing representative samples for qualitative research, Schofield suggests that it is instead possible to develop a more appropriate conception of generalisability suitable for qualitative research in which the researcher chooses cases 'on the basis of their fit with a typical situation' rather than because of the common practice of convenience – indeed, multisite qualitative studies have become more common since the 1970s (ibid., pp. 209–211). Qualitative researchers may still find that they need to consider issues of sampling and sources of bias in order to ensure diversity if not representativeness. Therefore, we should not decide to take a qualitative approach purely because we 'cannot be bothered' to deal with the tediums of sampling and representativeness – qualitative research should still be rigorous; it is not an excuse for sloppy research.

As researchers, we still have to interpret what we find from our research and we have to make considered decisions to choose important information from the wealth of data we collect: how can we be absolutely sure that meanings are not lost or changed in this process? We have mentioned that a strength is that we get to know our research topic. What if we become too close or sympathetic and lose our objectivity? Imagine, for example, that you were researching a group who regularly participate in political violence. After many months of observing and talking to the members you actually begin to sympathise with their beliefs and even decide to become a member. This is referred to as 'going native' (Punch, 1993, p. 186). By 'going native' we lose our sense of detachment and become subject to selectivity and inaccuracy (Foster, 1996, p. 76), thereby undermining the validity of our research.

Using observational methods in political research

For some research questions it is necessary to do more than ask questions during a one-off encounter. Also, we might find that people act differently in an unfamiliar environment compared to a familiar one (referred to as *symbolic interactionism*). If we wish to learn anything about political behaviour in a particular context, we must also engage with that context and undertake what is referred to as participant observation.

The skills of observation help us to make sense of, and participate in, the world. It is, in fact, more appropriate to discuss observational research in terms of techniques, rather than a single technique: 'it may be used to obtain descriptive quantitative data on the incidence of particular sorts of behaviour or events . . . or to enable qualitative description of the behaviour or culture of a particular group, institution or community' (Foster, 1996, p. 58).

For the purposes of research, observational research can be 'systematic' (structured) or 'ethnographic' (less structured) (ibid., p. 57). The systematic approach is often associated with the positivist tradition of the social sciences; that is, we have precise definitions of observable behaviour which we can measure. We may count, for example, the number of occasions on which female members of a committee speak. We can again see that the traditional divisions between quantitative and qualitative research do not imply mutual exclusivity: the format of data is different, but the tools of acquiring the data are multipurpose, and the conclusions we reach using the two methods may – or may not – be identical.

In contrast, 'prolonged participant observation' has proved to be appropriate when researching organisations or movements which are generally highly secretive or isolated. This is exemplified by Punch's research of the police, in which prolonged participation allowed a sense of empathy 'with the norms, values and behaviour of that group' to develop (Punch, 1993, pp. 184–185). Rather than behaving as though there was a 'stranger in the ranks', the police officers Punch researched became more familiar and even trusting of their observer, and perhaps did or said things differently as the study progressed. However, as we identified in Briefing box 5.1, we need to be aware of potential problems when conducting observational research. To what extent does the observer remain independent – or does he/she 'go native'? How do we determine which actions are important?

It is important to bear in mind that when we talk about observational research we do not necessarily mean that all the researcher does is watch and take notes, remaining silent throughout many hours of research. Imagine how difficult it must feel to not ask a question, and how unnerving it must feel for those we are studying to be followed around be someone furiously scribbling notes and not breathing a word! However, in comparison to formal interviews, which may take place in a quiet room for a set length of time, we support what we see in observational research with data from conversations, discussions and, if appropriate, impromptu interviews (Foster, 1996, p. 83).

The advantage of an observational research approach is that we are not relying, for example, purely upon a political actor to tell us what rules and responsibilities their job entails; we can actually witness this ourselves. In contrast to relying upon interviews as a means of extrapolating data, observation can record events 'as they happen', and this can provide a rich source of data which support other data gained from interviews, documents and statistics (Dargie, 1998, p. 66). The main advantages of using observation as a research tool are that: the importance of context can be considered (do elites behave differently in different types of meetings?); it helps us to understand the way in which decisions are made (is it by a group or by an individual?); it helps us to understand process and practice (are certain members of a political group expected to attend all meetings?); and it is useful in the analysis of behaviour (who takes charge in a meeting?). We have already hinted that people are not always willing to discuss deeply personal political issues. Observing political behaviour can prove to be more illuminating than a formal interview. As a result,

---

Briefing box 5.2 Advantages and disadvantages of observational research

Advantages

- Directly recorded by the observer rather than relying on others;
- provides supplementary data to surveys and interviews;
- observer may 'see' relevant factors which the observed cannot;
- gleans information which others cannot or may not wish to discuss.

Disadvantages

- Accessibility may be difficult or impossible;
- reactivity;
- relies upon interpretations made by the observer;
- time-consuming, costly and potentially unrepresentative;
- cannot guide the discussion/behaviour of those being studied;
- locating a suitable site.

those using observation should appreciate the privileged access they are being given to research subjects and documents.

However, we should also appreciate that observational research has its weaknesses. Replication (as a means of checking validity) may be possible for systematic, but not ethnographic, observations (Foster, 1996, p. 90). Perhaps the most challenging concern facing political researchers wishing to employ observational research is that of gaining access. The generally secretive nature of the British political system means that we are not likely to find it easy to sit in on ministerial meetings, or observe the Prime Minister during a 'typical day's work'. Very careful consideration should be given to the method(s) of data collection and the research design by those wishing to gain access to political elites (Dargie, 1998, p. 66). Added to this, the process of organisation (never mind the actual observation itself) can be extremely time-consuming, requiring the researcher to be flexible (not only in terms of when observations can actually take place, but also in being aware that last-minute cancellations can occur): 'it is a high-risk strategy' (ibid., p. 67). Flexibility is also important in relation to other aspects of carrying out fieldwork. Observing decision makers may be very frustrating if the researcher only has access to some meetings (due to issues of confidentiality). If, for example, your research entailed 'shadowing' an MP, you may discover that particular surgery meetings have to be conducted in private. In addition, we have to rely upon what actually happens rather than generating 'interesting scenarios'. If what sounded like an important meeting in fact turns out to be extremely dull and uninformative, this is just bad luck!

Dargie also raises the issue of *reliability*: it may take a long period of observation to be able to recognise 'normal' patterns and trends. Whilst observations which last a week may provide a wealth of data, we may not be able to acknowledge how 'typical' that week is of usual behaviour/activities (for example, might an elite select a week in which they are involved in an unusually high number of policy meetings?). There is, of course, the possibility that the subject of the study behaves differently because he/she is aware of being observed – known as '*reactivity*' (Foster, 1996, p. 88).

Observation may take the form of a preliminary research stage – a form of pilot research – or may be used at the end of a project to supplement other methods. Therefore, difficult as it may be to envisage scenarios where observation can be used in political research, we should not dismiss observational research as either untenable or inappropriate. In comparison to the types of studies we discussed in Part I, we cannot realistically expect to carry out large-scale studies – in Dargie's (1998) study there were only eight cases.

Finally, we must give some consideration to the ethical duties of the researcher: should people be observed for studies without their knowledge or consent? It is not, after all, unusual to read studies which refer to 'a Northern Labour MP' or 'a former group activist'. For example, if we are observing political behaviour at public meetings permission may not be an issue, but the same is not true in more private scenarios. In fact, in order to access a position for observational research one will probably already have had to deal with 'gatekeepers' – those in positions of authority who have the power to grant or withhold access (Foster, 1996, pp. 64–66). How should confidential information be treated? Heclo and Wildavsky (1974) stress that observational research requires an atmosphere of 'mutual trust'. It is important that researchers 'place' themselves – that is, admit who they are and why the study is being conducted (Finch, 1993, p. 172), as covert studies can create all sorts of problems (see Fielding, 1982, outlined below).

Despite these potential difficulties, those involved in observational research should practice *reflexivity* (the 'continual monitoring of, and reflection on, the research process') and *triangulation* (using different data and methods to uncover the same results as a way of ensuring validity) (Foster, 1996, p. 91). Before we progress to an assessment of the issues central to conducting good qualitative interviews in the next chapter, we shall conclude here by briefly outlining some 'classic' examples of qualitative political studies.

Case studies of qualitative research in political science

We have discussed in earlier chapters some of the established sources of quantitative political data (for example, the Essex Data Services), yet in comparison, there is a much smaller reserve of qualitative political research. It would be easy to say that relatively little has been collected by this approach, but this would not be a fair justification. In terms of general access to existing qualitative data, there are practical issues surrounding the 'openness' of such data as gathered by interviews and observations. Perhaps the most central is the maintenance of anonymity for those studied: far less qualitative political research would exist if participants could not be guaranteed confidentiality. However, existing sources are available. The Qualidata Centre (again at Essex) was established in 1994: 'with the aims of making available to researchers a centrally held list of the location of qualitative primary sources and facilitating their deposit in existing archives' (Bale, 1996, p. 66). In addition, since the 1980s there has been a great increase in the availability of computer-aided techniques of qualitative analysis, such as the computer packages CAQDAS (Computer Assisted Qualitative Data Analysis), NUD*IST and ETHNOGRAPH.

Observing political activity

The types of observational research we have discussed in this chapter are relatively underused in political research, and this is partly to do with the fact that the success of observational methods may be limited by access. Dargie (1998) successfully employed observational techniques as part of her examination of the activities of chief executives, stating that it 'sheds light on new aspects of political behaviour and political actors' (p. 66).

Fielding (1982) combined the methods of interviewing and observation to conduct his research on the National Front. In order to gain reliable data, he took on the role of an 'unconverted sympathiser' in order 'to understand why NF members believe what they do, and to examine the link between their ideology and their actions in an extreme right-wing racial-nationalist political movement' (p. 81). The advantages of attending branch meetings and marches as well as conducting interviews allowed Fielding to develop an understanding of the 'language of motives' that National Front members used to legitimate their political actions. As we noted earlier, qualitative interviewing allows for greater expression, and Fielding found 'the most important answers often arose from casual asides, rather than the interview schedule' (p. 87).

Exploring the political mind

Lane's American study entitled *Political Ideology* (1962) employed a series of unstandardised interviews with fifteen men over a seven-month period in order to develop an appreciation of 'the latent political ideology of the American urban common man' and the extent to which this ideology 'supports or weakens the institutions of democracy' (p. 3). Lane chose not to rely on volunteers for this project (the weaknesses of volunteer samples are dealt with in Chapter 2) but rather selected names randomly from a list of voters in one particular housing development. This enabled Lane to compare the attitudes and beliefs of a group of men who shared several basic similar characteristics, as acceptance into the housing development was dependent upon marital status and level of income. What resulted from this approach were deeply 'biographical' accounts (ibid., p. 10).

Who has power?

Qualitative research methods are seen as the most appropriate means of researching the issue of who holds political power. In *The Private Government of Public Money*, Heclo and Wildavsky (1974) outlined two aims of their research. First, they wished to explain the expenditure process as it operates in British central government, and second, they used the expenditure process to demonstrate the characteristic practices of British central government in relation to the availability of funding and the process of public policy making.

Heclo and Wildavsky claim that previous research on public spending has tended to be historical, and in contrast they chose qualitative methods as a means of carrying out a contemporary study. By interviewing and observing civil servants, ministers and MPs in detail they were able to analyse the process of negotiation among officials, and the nature of bargaining that occurred. Heclo and Wildavsky's justification for their approach was:

> How can we penetrate the work-a-day world of these political men? . . . To understand how political administrators behave we must begin by seeing the world through their eyes . . . The world does look different depending on whether the participant is in Parliament or Government, spending Department or Treasury . . . The participant is the expert on what he does; the observer's task is to make himself expert on why he does it.
>
> (Ibid., p. xvii)

Heclo and Wildavsky acknowledge that there are limitations to what can be asked of civil servants and politicians, and as a result they refrained from asking about current cases and personalities. After conducting over 200 'extensive and intensive' interviews with various relevant individuals, Heclo and Wildavsky concluded that the expenditure process revolved around mutual dependency between these groups of people, and whilst many of those studied were very helpful, some respondents felt that researchers could never really understand what they did (p. xxii). In relation to our earlier comments about the limitations of qualitative methods, we are still relying upon a researcher's interpretation of political activity, and as such cultural relativism may still be misunderstood.

Explanations of voting behaviour

Your studies so far may have led you to the presumption that there is only one way to study mass political behaviour (for example, voting), and that is via quantitative methods. Indeed, in Chapter 2 we looked at the important role of the British Election Studies. However, although quantitative methodology certainly dominates electoral studies, we should not ignore or undermine the role that qualitative methods may also contribute to this area of study. Devine (1994, p. 215) argues that the bias towards quantitative methods has led to 'theoretical conservatism and the dominance of a system-biased approach in voting behaviour', whilst 'intensive interviewing techniques . . . allow people to account for their political attributes and behaviour in ways which they find subsequently meaningful'. The 'theoretical conservatism' that Devine refers to is prevalent in the fact that studies of voting behaviour have tended to focus upon the existence of certain *variables*, such as social class, occupation and car ownership. Devine, however, suggests that even this information does not go 'deep' enough, as highly structured interviews leave little opportunity for us to understand 'individual biographies' – the lessons of family life, educational achievements, work experience and patterns of social mobility which help to explain personal interests (ibid., p. 219).

Devine's *Affluent Workers Revisited* is one of a small number of qualitative studies analysing voting behaviour. During 1986–7 Devine employed semi-structured interviews to study Vauxhall car plant workers and their wives in Luton. Devine's study was underpinned by two research questions: did members of the working class lead privatised life styles, and to what extent did life style influence attitudes and voting behaviour? The benefits of this, according to Devine, is that such interview formats: 'allow the interviewees to develop their own concepts and arguments, making it unnecessary to infer causal links and consistencies between perceptions, feelings, meanings, attitudes and behaviour' (Devine, 1992a, p. 162). That is, interviewees could explain their political preferences in language they were familiar with, in relation to issues important in their lives and not according to pre-set themes and expectations as dictated by the researcher.

Devine encountered problems generating a study sample because of poor industrial relations at that time, and thus relied on snowballing (explained in Chapter 2). The study generated a sample of thirty-two working-class couples from a range of backgrounds (emphasising the importance of studying different cases rather than using survey-style probability sampling). This study was particularly important because the research asked workers not only about class differences, but also what they understood terms such as working class and middle class to mean.

The *Affluent Workers Revisited* study benefited from the use of qualitative interviews because Devine found 'unanticipated contextual issues'. For example, she did not expect race to be important, but found it was in terms of: (a) the sense of local community; (b) its frequent perception as playing a role in the unequal distribution of resources (such as jobs and housing); and (iii) the interpretation by supporters of different parties of the issue of race in different ways to support their political beliefs (Devine, 1994, pp. 221–223). Devine discovered through interviews that class awareness was not as clear or coherent as many prominent theorists had suggested, and, as a result, claimed that the class dealignment theory of voting behaviour was not wholly appropriate in the late 1980s (partly because the rise in home ownership had made class distinction more difficult). As a result, working-class Conservative electoral support derived from disillusionment with the Labour Party

(Devine, 1992, p. 170). Similar findings were uncovered by Labour Party research after the 1992 election (see the earlier comments in this chapter on focus groups).

An aspect to which we need to pay close attention in qualitative research is how do we know that our findings are 'important'? Remember, in the section on ethnography in this chapter, we stated that there is a difference between general trends and significant findings. How was Devine able to conclude that race was 'important' in terms of party support? Could it be that in fact she was intentionally (or even unconsciously) directing the interview towards this issue? Devine reinforces her conclusions by stating that it was the interviewees who raised the issue 'at least twice' in the interview, and that the issue was raised in relation to changes in the larger and more local community of Luton. The issues of potential interviewer effect will be discussed in more detail in Chapter 6.

Political selection

Norris and Lovenduski (1995), as part of the 1992 British Candidate Study, employed qualitative techniques to analyse party candidate views on selection procedures. The study included detailed one-hour interviews with thirty-nine MPs, candidates and applicants, along with observations of selection meetings. These qualitative data were used in addition to data gleaned from over 3000 surveys, official documentation (such as party constitutions), voter surveys and demographic constituency data (pp. 16–17), in order to develop an understanding of the legislative recruitment process; that is, why do some political aspirants succeed and climb the career ladder whilst others do not? A similar theme was researched by Levy (1996), who employed a mixture of interviews and surveys in order to develop an understanding of Labour MPs' attitudes towards the modernisation process and Clause Four reform, and in particular an insight into the factors which might influence attitudes. Levy suggests that aggregate survey data demonstrated that MPs were highly supportive of modernisation, whilst the qualitative data showed some reservations to this:

> An examination of the words behind the opinions shows that, while a significant number of MPs are strongly supportive of party reform, a number expressed support in pragmatic terms, suggesting their support was because of the negative public relations which would have resulted from the changes not being implemented once initiated.
>
> (Ibid., p. 190)

Therefore, whilst support for party modernisation was in evidence, the *reasons* were more varied, and Levy could identify what we might call 'negative' and 'positive' support – the fallout of not supporting reform was perceived by some MPs as being far more damaging than any reform itself.

Conclusion

So far we have considered why and when we may apply qualitative research tools in political research. This is to some extent determined by what we are researching – it is not always feasible or appropriate to ask people to fill in questionnaires. Second, it is also determined by the type of data we wish to accrue – particularly if we are interested in the 'why' rather than the 'what'. It can be useful, to use the words of Burns (2000, p. 298), when 'one must look beyond the "public" and "official" versions of reality in order to examine the unacknowledged or tacit understandings as well'.

We have shown some of the general strengths and weaknesses of employing a qualitative approach, focused upon the use of observational techniques, and have considered some 'classic' political studies using qualitative research. This is not to imply that quantitative and qualitative research never mix. Rather, we have suggested that they often work as contrasting or supplementary research tools, equally capable of tackling the same research question. Indeed, researchers often employ both techniques as a process of triangulation. The main strengths of employing qualitative methods in political research are that they illustrate 'multi-causal processes which shape political attitudes and behaviour in a particular time and place' (Devine, 1994, p. 223). In the next chapter we shall focus upon the practical issues affecting interviewing.

Further reading

D. Marsh and G. Stoker, *Theory and Methods in Political Science* London: Macmillan, 1995, chs 7 and 8, provide a good introduction to the differences between quantitative and qualitative research in politics.

For a more detailed explanation of focus group methodologies, see J.B. Mannheim and R.C. Rich, *Empirical Political Analysis: Research Methods in Political Science*, 4th edn, New York: Longman, 1995, ch. 20.

For a more detailed analysis of the advantages of using qualitative methods for studying political attitudes, see F. Devine, 'Working-class Evaluations of the Labour Party', in I. Crewe, P. Norris, D. Denver and D. Broughton (eds), *British Elections and Parties Yearbook 1991*, Hemel Hempstead: Harvester Wheatsheaf, 1992, and her 'Learning More About Mass Political Behaviour: Beyond Dunleavy', in D. Broughton, D. Farrell, D. Denver and C. Rallings (eds), *British Elections and Parties Yearbook 1994*, London: Frank Cass, 1994. C. Dargie 'Observation in Political Research', *Politics*, 18 (1) (1994): 65–71, provides a useful guide to employing observational methods for political research.

Chapter 6

Conducting interviews in political research

Lisa Harrison and Wolfgang Deicke

Introduction

In Chapter 3 we looked at some of the practical considerations that you will need to be aware of if you are to carry out surveys. Here, we shall take a similar approach to the use of interviews as a qualitative research tool. One aspect we need to establish is the difference between a survey and an interview. It is possible to explore the same research question with both techniques, although one tool may be more appropriate than the other depending upon: facilities (such as time and money); sampling criteria and the population we are researching; and the type of data we wish to uncover.

Seale (1998) claims that the rise in the use of qualitative interview methods has developed as a result of interpretivist criticisms of the 'classical approach to interviews'. The interpretivists observed several key problems with questionnaires. The first is that what people say is not necessarily what really happens in practice. Remember in Chapter 3 we referred to Bartle's analysis of the British Elections Studies, in which it was claimed that a particular design fault is question ordering, leading to an inflated reporting of strength of party identification. A second problem with questionnaires is that attempts to standardise the meanings of responses is 'doomed to failure'. Third, questionnaires have the potential to be 'exploitative'. This was a criticism levelled, in particular, by feminist social researchers who identified that 'an unequal, unbalanced relationship was thereby set up, where the researcher possessed all the power to define what was relevant and what was irrelevant', enabling a focus upon specific topics and agenda setting at the cost of other concerns (ibid., pp. 204–205). However, we should not assume that qualitative interviews cannot be undermined by interviewer effects (as will be discussed later).

Qualitative interviews do not merely provide an alternative to questionnaires. A further potential benefit is that interviews facilitate our ability to glean information not recorded in documents elsewhere, or indeed allow us to develop our interpretation of existing documents, relevant events and personalities (ibid., p. 8). In this chapter we shall look at the common characteristics of qualitative interviews (including what we refer to as elite interviews), when it is appropriate to use interviews in political research, some potential concerns we should address, and relate these issues to a detailed case study of recent research into the far right.

What is an interview?

An interview is an encounter between a researcher and a respondent, where the respondent's answers provide the raw data. Stedward (1997, p. 151) claims:

> In particular, the interview is a great vehicle for bringing a research topic to life. It is also an excellent method of obtaining data about contemporary subjects which have not been extensively studied and for which there is little literature.

We shall focus here upon four particular concerns that all researchers face: what to ask; how to save the data; how to ensure reliability; and last but not least, who to ask. In Chapter 9 we shall address a fifth issue: how to integrate interview material into your own research. Just as we can ask survey respondents to tick boxes or give short answers, we can also conduct interviews using different *schedules*. An interview schedule refers to the questions we ask, in terms of the order (or lack of it) and the wording of questions (Wilson, 1996, p. 94). Here, we distinguish between three theoretical types of schedules: standardised; semi-standardised; and unstandardised. It has been common elsewhere to refer to structured and unstructured interviews; however, as Wilson claims, the phrase 'unstructured' is a misnomer implying that it just happens without any consideration or planning, and as such the term naturalistic would be more appropriate (ibid., p. 98). Stedward (1997, p. 152) goes a stage further by criticising the whole process of categorising interview schedules as 'simplistic', claiming that: 'rather there is a continuum from which researchers select lines of enquiry, seeking open or closed responses to a greater or lesser degree', which is probably a fair reflection of the realities, rather than the theory, of research. For example, when we ask a question such as: '*What were the major reasons for you joining pressure group X?*', we are unlikely to say: '*and tell me in no more than one sentence*'. Likewise, if someone did give a very short answer, we are just as unlikely to say: '*Is that all you have to say?*' Rather, depending upon whether we require quantitative or qualitative data, we shall ask precise or general questions and choose which material it is most important to record. Therefore, in order to appreciate the appropriateness of interview types we shall consider interviews in relation to schedules. Briefing box 6.1 identifies some key differences.

In the case of the *standardised interview*, we ask every question in the same way. This is similar in principle to a survey, and indeed we often produce data which can easily be turned into a quantifiable form. For example, in a survey we may ask a young person the question: '*Do you discuss politics at home?*' For quantitative purposes we might have categories of 'yes', 'no' or 'occasionally', although this latter category in particular is very broad and is open to varying interpretations by different respondents. By collecting the data in their qualitative form, however, we might gain very different responses to the same basic category: 'Occasionally – when a particular news story sparks off a discussion', as opposed to 'Occasionally – my Dad and his brother often argue about politics but we all think they're boring and leave them to it'. The former response implies a much more active involvement in political discussions at home than the latter response. Quantifying verbatim answers is not unfeasible but can be time-consuming. We often lose some of the information's *quality* by quantification, or end up with so many categories that quantification is

---

Briefing box 6.1 The classification of interview schedules

Schedule type	Standardised	Semi-standardised	Unstandardised
Example	Surveys Opinion polls	Focus groups Large-scale studies	In-depth studies Oral/life histories
Interview style	Least conversational	→	Most conversational

Source: Adapted from Burns (2000, p. 423)

of little overall value. Therefore, once we move beyond asking basically factual questions and request explanations ('Why do you prefer party leader x to party leader y?') we shall probably find that qualitative responses are the most interesting and useful. Yet by following a standardised interview we still have comparable data.

In comparison, a *semi-standardised interview* combines quantitative questions (such as age, gender), but can generate more qualitative data as the interviewer seeks clarification and elaboration of answers. Therefore, as the interview progresses the schedule allows for some level of probing. We discussed in Chapter 5 the example of focus groups. The focus group moderator will prompt the discussion with certain questions and maintain the central theme of the discussion, but it is important for interviewees to be allowed to explain their beliefs and feelings. The reasons for requiring qualitative data are much the same as we explained for standardised interviews: we are interested in knowing the 'whys' and 'hows' as well as the 'whats'. It is still important that we have comparable information, which might, for example, enable us to differentiate types of responses along the lines of age, gender and social status.

Our third category is the *unstandardised interview* – also referred to as an informal, focused, unstructured, or free interview. An unstandardised interview takes the form of 'a free-flowing conversation, relying heavily on the quality of the social interaction between the investigator and informant, that can be subtly redirected by the interviewer if it should stray too far off the track of the research study' (Burns, 2000, p. 425). The aim is to provide qualitative, detailed data, and the structure allows for greater flexibility and discovery of meaning. That is, we ask questions as and when they are appropriate, not because we have asked them of others, and we choose the wording as is appropriate, because 'people's responses are highly sensitive to different forms of question wording' (Dunleavy, 1990, p. 457). As we progress from standardised to unstandardised interviews we require fewer formalised questions. Instead, many qualitative interviewers make use of an *aide-mémoire*, that is, a brief list of topics to be covered, though not in any particular order (Burns, 2000, p. 428; Seale, 1998, p. 206) (see Briefing box 6.2). This helps to ensure that the interview remains focused, without actually undermining the flow of the discussion.

Briefing box 6.2 Example of an interview *aide-mémoire*

1 When did you first become aware of Party X?
2 Why Party X and not another political party?
3 First contact with party?
4 Level of involvement/activity?
5 Part of, or distinct from, wider social network?
6 Changes in attitude/participation?

Source: Adapted from Seale (1998, p. 206)

We can see that this is not a strict set of questions, but 'themes' which the interviewer would ideally like to cover. You may find that the interview progresses naturally from one theme to the next, but the *aide-mémoire* can help you to keep on track if time is limited.

If we consider Lane's (1962) interviews (as briefly mentioned in Chapter 5) we can recall that they adopted a strongly conversational format. In order to build up mutual trust between himself and the interviewee, Lane gradually guided discussions away from the 'general' (broad policy issues such as trade unionism, foreign policy, war and poverty) to more 'personal' issues (such as discussing political parties, family experiences and occupational information) in later meetings (p. 7).

One issue to which we must pay attention is the procedure for recording qualitative interview data. Whereas in surveys we have a list of questions with tick-box or short answers, the same does not apply to focused interviews. Unless you are very good at shorthand, the chances are that you will only be able to make brief notes during a semi- or unstandardised interview. However, even this can undermine the quality of an interview as your energies are consumed with scribbling in a notepad rather than actually *listening* to what is being said. It may also mean that you are unlikely to have any substantial verbatim quotes. The ideal alternative is to tape-record interviews, although you should make sure you have high-quality equipment. Again, if we refer back to Lane's (1962, p. 9) study: 'By the use of a tape recorder the interviews provided a *textual* account of everything said. The choice of words employed, the hesitations between words, the style and language of discourse were all revealed in the transcript.' Mannheim and Rich (1995, p. 167) describe the tape-recording of interviews as a 'controversial tool', which is not without problems – either because some interviewees will not grant permission to be recorded or because the recorded interview is not of a transcribable quality. Even if we can tape-record an interview, we must be particularly careful regarding the giving of permission to use the information – by the interviewer and/or by other researchers (Seldon, 1988, p. 12). One simple approach we can take is to hide the interviewee's identity by using terms such as 'interviewee one', or by simply swapping real names for alternatives (but keep note of the changes for your own purposes).

In Chapter 3, we stated that surveys vary in length and structure depending upon the form of information we require (be it facts, perceptions, opinions, attitudes or behavioural reports). Similar opportunities are faced when we choose to employ a qualitative interviewing approach, in that the procedure and questioning techniques should differ depending upon the nature of the study and the character of the respondents (Mannheim and Rich, 1995, p. 156). Stedward (1997), for example, employed interviews to research the influence of anti-racism on British public policy, and conducted interviews with a range of people which included anti-racist activists, office bearers and officers of interest groups, civil servants, MPs and MEPs. The precise interview questions varied depending upon the particular interviewee.

Reliability (and, as a result, validity) are underlying concerns when conducting qualitative interviews. According to Seldon (1988, p. 3), interviews offer 'always an inferior source of information to documents written at the time' but nevertheless provide an 'essential stop-gap' as access to documents can be severely limited, particularly when researching contemporary history. For example, texts on the Falklands War could not have been written for at least 30 years without the resource of interviews. Added to this: 'Interviews can be particularly helpful in fleshing out documents when it comes to reconstructing the roles and methods of personalities, and their relationships with others' (ibid., p. 4).

Interviews may also help in the process of identifying which documents have been deemed to be important, read and acted upon. Added to this, interviews can fill gaps in the documentation, particularly as we have seen a decline in letter writing and the keeping of diaries. We can, of course, ensure that what we record is as accurate as possible via the process of *respondent validation*: by sending a written copy of the interview to the interviewee for checking (Walsh, 1998, p. 231; also, see case study below).

Referring back to Heclo and Wildavsky's (1974) study of public spending (outlined in Chapter 5), we noted that the researchers identified that only a particular group of individuals held the relevant knowledge of public spending (politicians and civil servants) whilst the general public held relatively little knowledge or interest. If we were to research political party dynamics, for example, the questions we ask of elites may be very different in nature to the questions we ask of ordinary party members (see the case study in this chapter). As such the *status* of those we interview is a much more central concern in our research design than it would be when conducting quantitative surveys.

Elite interviewing

If we wish to discover how political institutions operate, how important decisions are made and how political power is attained, we are not likely to ask the public at large, but rather those individuals (very often a small group) who have access to this level of information – those referred to as political elites. Richards (1996, p. 199) defines elites as 'those in exposed or important positions'. As we have mentioned in the previous chapter, a potential problem for research of this nature may be access, and even successful elite interviews are likely to be based upon a small sample of non-representative participants. However, representative sampling is not as central as in quantitative research because 'Elite interviewers have to assume that potential respondents differ in how much they can contribute to the study and that each respondent has something unique to offer' (Mannheim and Rich, 1995, p. 164). Therefore, whilst the information gleaned is likely to be a highly subjective account of an event or issue, the primary role of an elite interview is to provide an insight into the mind of that particular political actor.

Richards (1996) assesses the value of elite interviewing in terms of several advantages and disadvantages. The advantages are: they may help with the interpretation of documents and reports (especially if we are interviewing the actual author); they may help with the interpretation of personalities; they provide information which may not be recorded elsewhere; and they can help in establishing contact networks and access to others (that is, they act as a method of snowball sampling). However, we must also bear in mind that the limitations of access affect the overall representativeness of any research findings, whilst the reliability of the information gleaned may be questionable (interviewees could supply inaccurate information both intentionally and unintentionally) or impossible to substantiate (ibid., p. 200). The reliability of interviewees is something we should always consider. While information may be inaccurate for very genuine reasons (memory lapse), interviewees may also be unreliable for ulterior reasons (because they have an axe to grind or wish to portray themselves in a positive light).

Perhaps the most challenging issue we confront when conducting elite interviews is 'where to start' – or, put another way, who to interview and when. The status of particular interviewees may mean that we find out something particularly enlightening when we are conducting interview number five which, had we known it earlier, may have led us to ask more probing questions of interviewees one to four. Indeed, as Mannheim and Rich (1995) suggest, elite interviewing is a 'process of discovery', and later interviews will often be more useful than the earliest ones. As a result, they suggest that central figures should be interviewed later in the study, and that:

> If possible, it is best to avoid interviewing first the mavericks, opposition leaders, persons thought to have extreme views, or leaders of any dominant coalition, because word of this may be passed to other interviewees and make them hostile or defensive.
>
> (Ibid., pp. 164–165)

Richards (1996) suggests that elite interviews are most productive if carried out in the latter stages of research, and has found that civil servants make the best interviewees, whilst ex-politicians can make the worst (see also Seldon, 1988, p. 10). If requests for interviews are refused, try to establish why: will that person never give an interview? are they 'too busy'? or are they concerned by confidentiality issues? It may be possible to 'talk people round' but do not be pushy – it is they who are giving you valuable help, not usually the other way around.

In terms of identifying potential interviewees, it is worth locating (up-to-date) reference lists. When conducting research into the influence of anti-racism on public policy, Stedward (1997) located potential interviewees through sources such as *The Civil Service Yearbook*, *The European Union Institutions Yearbook* and *Dod's Parliamentary Companion*. Potential sources of existing interviews are the British Sound Archive and the Oral History Society (Seldon, 1988, p. 13). Of course, once you have conducted your first interview it may be possible to gain access to more interviewees by word of mouth and recommendation. We suggest you read this case study in the chapter to learn more about the process of conducting interviews.

Some practical concerns

It may seem from what has been said so far that obtaining suitable interviewees is the hard part of the research process. While recruiting willing subjects for study may indeed be by no means problem-free, there are other issues surrounding qualitative interviewing which also must be considered. Finch (1993) claims that interviewing raises numerous methodological, personal, political and moral issues. For example, Oakley found that an informal interview style conducted in the home was the most appropriate approach for interviewing women as it avoids the participants feeling as though a hierarchical relationship exists (in Finch, 1993, p. 166). The belief that home environments produce the most productive interviews is also supported by Seldon (1988). Seale (1998, p. 209), however, points out that this supposed strength of unstandardised interviews does not automatically ensure that valid data will be obtained.

As with other research approaches, successful interviews have certain basic requirements (see Briefing box 6.3). In relation to *accessibility*, we have already considered how we might gain access to relevant interviewees. Many of the people we hope to interview are very busy and an interview request is unlikely to be unique. We have already made reference to snowballing as one method of sampling frequently used in qualitative research, for example, interviewees nominate other potential interviewees (see, for instance, the work of Devine in Chapter 5, and also Stedward, 1995). In Chapter 5 we suggested that a common obstacle we face when conducting qualitative research is the control of access through 'gatekeepers': 'Gatekeepers are the sponsors, officials and significant others who have the power to grant or block access to and within a setting' (Walsh, 1998, p. 221).

Maintaining *objectivity* is important, as the nature of the interview usually means that the interviewer is not as distant from the interviewee as in quantitative research. As with observation methods, this may lead to a sense of partisanship where the interviewer becomes less objective in reporting his/her findings, and we should strive to ensure that this does not occur.

Interviewer effects may also influence the objectivity of our research. The phrasing of questions is just as important in qualitative research as we have shown it to be when conducting surveys. The language we use should be as objective as possible, and interviewer bias can mean that particular opinions are seen as desirable. If a trend does appear (as in Devine's study outlined in Chapter 5), try to show that this was not an interviewing effect

Cognition is vital because it is important that the interviewee understands what is required of him or her. The interviewee must have access to the relevant information, otherwise there is an 'understanding gap' which creates expected rather than realistic answers. Of course, people may be reluctant to answer questions for a range of personal, political or ethical reasons. This is particularly important when conducting political research. The very word 'politics' can trigger a range of reactions among different people. For example, Lane (1962, p. 171) comments that, for one of his interviewees, '[Rapuano] thinks only of politics when he thinks of government.' During a focus group with local sixth formers, we found that the participants initially indicated 'no interest' in politics, yet then went on to discuss in some detail their

---

Briefing box 6.3 Requirements for successful interviews

- Accessibility;
- objectivity;
- cognition;
- motivation.

feelings on a range of issues which could easily have been classed as political. We have already stated that interviewees may fabricate responses. A simple fabricated response is bad enough, but one that is then expanded upon is even worse.

The purpose of the interview should be made clear. In an ideal situation we should be completely honest about the reasons for the interview – and in practice this may be more feasible than in some of the cases of participant observation that were discussed in Chapter 5. Thus, informing a potential interviewee about the nature of the study 'establishes credibility and improves the chances that respondents will agree to the interview' (Mannheim and Rich, 1995, p. 156). Indeed, even if we are carrying out a relatively large-scale interview project, then a short, standardised explanation of the study is very useful.

Just as we would pilot a survey, we can also do the same with an interview schedule. Whilst this helps us to identify ambiguous questions, in the qualitative arena it is perhaps more important for checking the length of time that an interview schedule requires to be completed (Stedward, 1997, p. 155). Do think carefully about what you can expect to find out in an hour, particularly if you are asking people to recall events from some time back. Interviewees may request a few moments to think about an unexpected question and, while this is helpful in attaining accurate and honest answers, it will inevitably eat up precious minutes.

(4) The fourth criterion we identified for a successful interview is *motivation*: that is, the interviewee's replies must be seen as valued. It is crucial that we maintain an interest in the interview (see the case study in this chapter). In Chapter 3 we identified some common problems which occur due to poor survey structure and wording. Similarly, these are rules which apply to questions we might wish to ask in a qualitative interview. For example, try to use short, precise questions and try to avoid ambiguous ones ('*Did you vote in the last election?*' – which one: local election, general election, committee election . . . ?). We should also remember not to asked 'loaded' questions which hint that particular forms of political behaviour or beliefs are good or bad – this may be approval/disapproval of political figures or evoking the belief that not voting is evading civic duty. A further problem may arise from research into particular fields where the researcher may use language that the interviewee does not understand (stilted language), or from attempting to research sensitive subjects, such as racial bigotry (Mannheim and Rich, 1995, pp. 157–160). However, the positive side to this is that, if it is a subject which the interviewee feels is important, some interviews may provide access to personal archives and a whole world of previously untouched material (Stedward, 1997, p. 157; see also Seldon, 1988, ch. 1).

Seldon (ibid.) identifies three challenges to the validity of employing interviews as a research tool. First is the limitations of memory, especially in relation to factual information. In comparison, interviews held too soon after the event may be 'clouded by personal impressions' (p. 6). Second, qualitative interviews inevitably involve unrepresentative sampling, although this can be avoided by 'drawing up systematic lists of potential interviewees from a wide variety of different organisations, backgrounds, sympathies, or whatever distinctions may be relevant' (p. 7). We have shown that Stedward (1997) attempted to explain the influence of anti-racism on public policy by interviewing individuals from a range of organisations.

The third problem is that qualitative interviewing can be time-consuming and costly. This is also supported by Stedward (ibid., p. 152) in her claim that: 'Aside from the time actually spent interviewing and travelling to the interview, you need to account for preparation, obtaining and setting up interviews, writing up and content analysis.' For Stedward, the optimal number of interviews in a single day was four. It is a good idea, she suggests, to employ interviews in the process of triangulation – that is, in conjunction with other methods, such as analysing archive material or participant observation.

Case study: using interviews in political research

Having established the theoretical advantages and shortcomings of qualitative methods in general (Chapter 5) and interviews in particular, we shall now turn to some of the more practical concerns. In the following, I shall use my experiences during research on the Austrian Freedom Party (FPÖ) in 1998–9 to illustrate some of the issues and problems which may confront you when choosing interviews as your research tool.

Theoretical concerns apart, the two questions which will inevitably determine every researcher's choice and – ideally – mix of methods are: 'What is it I want to find out?' and 'Which is the most appropriate way of obtaining that information?'.

In my case, these questions posed themselves during the initial literature review for a PhD on the loose working subject of 'right-wing extremism in Germany and Austria'. Two factors became clear quite quickly: first, at a practical level, that the literature on the Freedom Party stood in inverse relation to the party's mercurial rise in the polls throughout the 1980s. Second, at a more theoretical level, that much of the literature on the nature of the contemporary far right concentrated either on the social composition of the far right's electorate or on the party's respective leaders. In relation to the third piece of my puzzle, the party itself as the subject of investigation, the research tended to focus either on the parties' formal structure and constitution, or on their ideology as expressed in party programmes and literature. Certainly in the case of the FPÖ, next to nothing had been written on the party's members, activists and officials, or on the processes by which the party arrived at decisions over policy and strategy. Without such information, however, the various conflicting claims made about the party's nature (not that of its *electorate*, *programme* or *leader*) seemed a little 'leaky' at best. In the absence of any information on the availability of party internal documents (such as discussion papers, resolutions or protocols), interviews suggested themselves as the most obvious way of obtaining the information necessary to fill this gap in the literature.

What information can be gleaned from interviews?

At this point, it may be useful to introduce a further distinction in the information which can be obtained from interviewing party members. In qualitative research, all interviewees are regarded as 'experts', that is, they have information in which we as students or researchers are interested; at the same time, they may be experts on different aspects of party life and thus require slightly different treatment. Elite interviews with members higher up in the hierarchy may thus help us to gain an insight into party internal affairs, their views on the *role* and *importance* of ordinary party members, the decision making process, policy issues and the party's relations with its rivals and the media. The 'best' instrument at this level is the non-standardised 'guideline' interview, in which you simply structure the interview around a number of key points or issues tailored to your informant's specific 'expertise' or role in the party.

As pointed out earlier in this chapter, a possible drawback of elite interviews is that your subjects are usually very aware of their expert status and the fact that they are speaking 'as party representatives'. This, combined with the fact that they may also be more accustomed to being interviewed, could mean that it is more difficult to draw them on controversial issues. It also means that they might come to the interview with their own agenda. At any rate, to get the most mileage out of expert interviews and, just as importantly, to get along with your interviewees, it is vital that you do some background research beforehand and, where possible, cross-check the information conveyed for factual accuracy after the interview (unless they are very vain – it does happen! – they do not suffer fools gladly). My own experience here was very mixed: while some sleek professionals would not talk to me about anything beyond what they had previously decided to tell me, others were amazingly forthcoming.

The second, and for my purposes almost more important, group were the ordinary party members: they hold the key to understanding their political views and social concerns, their reasons for becoming involved, their perception of the party and its leadership. I also decided to interview some ex-members to establish their reasons for leaving the party and to gain some insight on internal party disputes. In contrast to the elite interviews, which usually result in data of a mixed quality (that is, 'subjective', in-depth interpretations of 'objective' events, and documents) and thus require careful cross-checking, 'subjectivity' is not a problem in interviews with ordinary members, but indeed the very thing you are looking for. To exemplify: if a party official tells me that the party's anti-foreigner stance was due to the fact that there are districts in Vienna where Austrians are becoming an endangered minority (as one of them did), then this claim would need checking. With the same claim from the mouth of an ordinary party member, the 'truth' or otherwise of such claims are of secondary importance; what matters here is that the respondent *feels* or *believes* this to be the case. A second important difference between the two levels of interviewing lies in the sample size: where the purpose of 'elite' interviews lies in contrasting, adding to and spicing up other available information, the purpose of interviews in the second case could range from the provision of illustrative case studies (in that case, a small sample will suffice) to attempts at developing some kind of 'typology' of members. As the aim here is to produce comparable data, the 'standardised' interview suggested itself as the best-suited approach. By asking all respondents the same question (and receiving similar or, indeed, very different answers), I did at least have an initial structure to the data, allowing me to draw up 'lists' of different reasons for joining/leaving the party and to search for patterns in the responses (for example, do women have different reasons than men for joining? had reasons changed over time?).

Access and sampling as problems

Working on the assumption (built on past experiences in the field) that right-wing parties are tightly controlled environments and have every reason to be suspicious of prying outsiders, I opted to approach the party through a gatekeeper – in my case a leading official of the Viennese FPÖ. While I wanted to 'enter' the party at the local level, I simultaneously approached members of the party's national executive, both because I wanted to interview them and because I hoped that their 'being informed' might work in my favour if the local party leadership sought reassurance or approval from above. In the event, once I had assuaged fears that I might be an undercover journalist, these measures proved superfluous, with the local party leadership being extremely helpful and supportive. After the initial interview with the leading party official, I asked him whether he or the party secretary could help me find a group of ten party members (an equal mix of men and women, preferably of different ages) who might be willing to be interviewed (an 'opportunity sample'). The risk here was, of course, that such a hand-picked sample could end up being highly biased towards the more respectable end of party politics – in other words, the party could 'choose' the way it wanted to present itself to me. As it turned out, this was not the case: the person in charge of selecting suitable candidates appeared to have made his choices on the basis of personal relations (calling in 'favours' from people he could approach), rather than with the party's image in mind. A brief counter-check in the archives of the anti-fascist *Dokumentationsarchiv des österreichischen Widerstandes* revealed that some of them were 'known' right-wingers with files of their own. I also received an invitation to a social function of two district branches, at which the party secretary introduced me to a number of other members and district officials. I made a point of asking each of my respondents at the end of the interview whether they knew of somebody else who might be willing to be interviewed (a snowballing strategy).

An alternative approach (which I used with very mixed results and only after I had become a 'known' face within the party) would be to write directly to members and, more importantly, ex-members who had stood as candidates for the party in local or national elections. This was possible due to the fact that their details are held and published in Vienna. (Note: At the level of local politics in Britain, practice varies between local authorities. Northampton Borough Council, for example, only keeps the details of candidates for six months after the local elections; thereafter the only records remaining are the names and parties of those elected.) The combination of both approaches netted a total of twenty-six interviews (four elite, five ex-elite, twelve members, five ex-members).

Setting up the interviews

Setting up the interviews was one of the most difficult parts of the research project. The elite interviews were usually held in offices, which could be busy. Most of my other respondents wanted to meet in public places. From a sociological observer's point of view, the ideal would have been to gain admission to the interviewees' homes, as this would provide further information on the respondent. Given the nature of my research topic, however, this was unlikely to happen and could also have been dangerous. Even though this turned out to be an unnecessary precaution in my case, I made a point in the early stages of the fieldwork of always letting someone else know what I was doing and who I was with. My advice is to let the interviewee choose a place they are comfortable with – but as quiet as possible. Public places may be inhibiting if interviewees' opinions are not exactly 'mainstream'. Here it proved that those whom I had approached directly had the least reservations about meeting me in private, presumably because I already knew where they lived and had 'invaded' their privacy by writing to them. In my experience, the point made earlier about the 'order' of arranging your interviews cannot be emphasised enough: the world of politics and politicians' networks was often smaller than I thought, and my 'experts' would often know who I had spoken to already, even if it was politicians from rival parties. I thus decided to leave interviews with ex-members and party renegades until the end of the fieldwork.

Conducting the interviews

How long does an interview take? Elite interviews were open-ended, but, as they took place during office hours, the interviewees would invariably be pushed for time, and sometimes arrived for interviews late, which could upset a tightly planned schedule or make the following interviews more strenuous. In comparison, with ordinary members the main problem was to find a mutually convenient time, usually in the afternoon or evening after work. This set a natural limit to the number of interviews I could carry out in a day. One should also not kid oneself as to how much one can do within a day – three interviews of forty-five to sixty minutes was my personal best; after this, I began to suffer from writer's cramp and my brain was struggling to function.

A word of warning here: it goes without saying that the quality of all interviews depends to a large degree upon the quality of the questions asked; the art here is to strike the right balance between a 'thematic focus' – what it is you really want to know – and a way of questioning that encourages your interviewees to abandon their reserve. Again, there is a difference in the way you should treat the 'party elite' and the ordinary membership. In order for interviews with the former to be most productive, a certain amount of critical probing and querying is necessary, otherwise you will end up with little more than the party's official position as already available in party literature and press interviews. It may, however, be in your interest not to be too critical in the first interviews if you are trying to 'soften up' somebody who can grant or deny you access to further party sources. In my case, I considered a 'lame' interview or two a price well worth paying.

While higher-ranking party officials were keenly aware of their public and expert status and interviews with them were conducted in a very professional atmosphere, some of the ordinary party members had doubts as to how and why their personal views and experiences should be important to anyone – never mind to a political scientist. I tried to counter this by pointing out at the beginning of the interview that it was their personal experiences and views I was interested in and that they should regard themselves as the experts in this situation. During the interviews, I found that some of the questions proved more difficult to answer than I had anticipated, as some of the respondents had either never really thought about it or had not been forced to articulate their motives to an outsider before. So, while the direct question *'Why did you become a member?'* is a perfectly fine 'open' question aimed at what you want to find out, it might give your interviewee the impression that you are after highly rationalised hard and fast 'reasons'. By rephrasing the question to something along the lines of *'I would like you to tell me how you became involved in politics'*, you allow your interviewee to give a softer, narrative approach which, with some further probing at appropriate points, could reveal a lot about both the influences *and* the reasons for their becoming involved, as well as detail of their political biography which might otherwise get lost (such as membership of other organisations, for example).

One of the most challenging tasks is the 'steering' or directing of the actual interview, that is, the social interaction above and beyond reading out your question to the interviewee. Your interviewees might try to second guess what it is you are after, what it is you want to hear, and try either to give or deny you that information. Again, a careful balance needs to be struck here between the methodological need to remain 'neutral' and the practicalities of getting a respondent to talk or cutting them short if they are going off at a tangent. Whilst I found it helpful to have thought about possible scenarios and developed strategies, you have to accept that you cannot prepare for everything. Some basic thumb rules do apply, though: if you want to 'steer' the discussion into a certain direction, you must *never* show your approval or disapproval of a voiced opinion, but signal your understanding or interest in a particular topic in more 'neutral' terms. Depending on your research topic, this can be very taxing at times, but it helps to remember that your interviewee is only telling you what you wanted to know and that, if you come across particularly objectionable views, this is the material that might spice up your dissertation. As a serious word of warning, though: close face-to-face involvement with your subjects means that this way of exploring controversial issues is not for the sensitive or faint-hearted.

Recording and transcribing the interviews

The most laborious part of the research process is the transcription process. Ideally, this should be done while the interview is still fresh in your head, and while you can still read the notes you made during the interview. Although this is not strictly speaking necessary if you are very good at note taking, you should also record the interviews, if only as evidence for posterity (or your supervisor). Recording the interviews is advisable for elite interviews, as it allows you to get the exact wording and distinguish between on- and off-the-record remarks (it might mean losing some of the 'juicier' quotes, but what is censored afterwards could prove interesting in itself). I found that the structured interviews with ordinary members lasted 45–90 minutes, with a 45-minute interview translating into roughly 13–16 typed pages of text and took me (a self-confessed two-finger typist) a day to transcribe using my notes and the tape recordings. That said, the transcription process for me proved crucial in that it allowed me to become 'familiar' with my data by milling over them time and again. This 'familiarity' – knowing off the top of your head who said what in response to which question – is what forms the basis of the subsequent data analysis.

Analysing and using the data

We have already discussed the different purposes of elite and 'member' interviews; while the former should be compared and contrasted with other, external information, the purpose of the latter is to discover patterns (differences and similarities) between and within the interviews. In both cases, however, the process of analysing your data should ideally take the form of a dialogue between you and your respondents: starting with your original question, for example, *'How did you become involved in politics?'*, you could begin by comparing the direct responses to that question, use them to formulate further questions: *'What are the factors or influences at work in members' political socialisation?'* and broaden your search for answers throughout the data. Another way of getting some structure into your data (depending on the size and nature of your sample) is to analyse your responses by demographic variables such as your respondents' age, sex, level of education, or along historical lines, such as their date of entry into the party (are there different 'generations' of joiners as well as different 'types'?). Ideally, each of these ways of organising your data should come up with a 'matrix' or mesh of connections (differences/similarities) between your interviews. The next step would be to try and connect these different layers of analysis, until you feel that you have exhausted your data. In most cases, this will not mean that you have found all the answers, but rather that the only questions left are those which your research raises, (but cannot answer).

In my experience as a supervisor of undergraduate dissertations in politics and sociology, using qualitative data to effect is one of the biggest problems facing the fledgling researcher. While most interviewers are capable of producing good, interesting data, the first reflex of less-experienced researchers is often to shove the transcripts of the interviews into an 'appendix' and make cursory references to them in the main body of the text, which is actually the worst you can do. Using qualitative interviews to effect means working with direct quotes extensively, in order to provide illustrative evidence for the 'themes' or 'typologies' generated by your research.

Ethics and anonymity

When coding your interviews, there are two issues you ought to bear in mind: first, in order to protect your informants and keep doors open for future generations of researchers, you should, where possible, make sure that your respondents cannot be identified (unless you have their explicit permission to do so). Normally, this does not present a problem, as you could give them codenames or refer to them anonymously by citing their job title and age (for example, *Hans, police officer, 35*). When interviewing party officials in their function as officials, or in cases where an interviewee's position in the party or public life is vital to what they are saying but makes them identifiable – there is, for example, little sense in giving the local party chairman a codename if a quote reveals his position – you should send them copies of the interview transcripts or the quotes you will be using and give them the option of deciding whether there are any passages which, with hindsight, they would rather were treated as 'off-the-record' remarks.

Second, particularly with 'anonymised' data, you should find a system of coding your data in a way which allows you (and your readers) to trace a quote back to the respective interview. The obvious thing here for standardised interviews would be to number the interviews as well as the questions (for example, *Hans, police officer, 35 I3/Q10*) to pinpoint your third interviewee's response to question number 10. There are no hard and fast rules, but your system ought to be consistent and clear.

Overview

With hindsight, my feelings on the interviewing process as part of the research project are mixed, with time proving to be the greatest constraint. Doing the research part-time, I only had three months for the fieldwork in Vienna. Getting myself set up there and introducing myself to the parties took a lot longer than anticipated, and by the time I felt that I was really 'in the field' and making contacts all the time, the three months were up, leaving me with the feeling that I did not get as much out of my fieldwork as I could have done. Apart from that, the interviews fulfilled their functions: talks with party official, their opposite numbers in rival parties and a series of academic and non-academic 'observers' of Freedom Party politics provided me with ample inside information and inspiration for new lines of enquiry. The standardised interviews with 'ordinary' members, after some initial tweaking with the wording of questions, also worked well and gave me a far better feel for understanding how the party works.

Conclusion

We have shown in this chapter that qualitative interviews form an important role in political research. While good interviews are guided by many of the principles relevant to good surveys (such as forward planning, representativeness, focus on the topic), there are both practical and strategic reasons why interviews are a valid alternative. The first concerns the type of information we wish to glean – either because it simply does not exist or because we require greater elaboration and explanations. We wish to know a person's beliefs, feelings and experiences from their perspective:

> Extended conversational interviews of this character provide an opportunity for *contextual* analysis. An opinion, belief, or attitude is best understood in the context of other opinions, beliefs, and attitudes, for they illuminate its meaning, mark its boundaries, modify and qualify its force.
>
> (Lane, 1962, p. 9)

Second, as we move from researching general opinions to requiring more specialised knowledge we inevitably reduce the size of our research population. Surveys become increasingly unsuitable as we research the experiences of experts and elites. By considering the interviewing experiences of one researcher's examination of the far right, we can begin to appreciate the central issues and concerns relevant to the operationalisation of good qualitative interviews in political science.

Further reading

A classic study of political attitudes is provided in R. Lane, *Political Ideology*, New York: Free Press of Glencoe, 1962, which provides an interview guide in Appendix A.

In terms of general practical issues surrounding the use of interviews, see J.B. Mannheim and R.C. Rich, *Empirical Political Analysis: Research Methods in Political Science* 4th edn, New York: Longman, 1995, ch. 8; and also C. Seale (ed.), *Researching Society and Culture*, London: Sage, 1998, ch. 16.

Both G. Stedward, 'On the Record: an Introduction to Interviewing', in P. Burnham (ed.), *Surviving the Research Process in Politics*, London: Pinter, 1997; and D. Richards, 'Elite Interviewing: Approaches and Pitfalls', *Politics*, 16 (3) (1996): 199–204, provide useful reflections of the value of interviews in researching political issues.

Chapter 7

Using existing resources in political research

Introduction

So far in this text we have focused upon collecting primary research data, whether in the form of quantitative or qualitative data. We have made some reference, albeit in a small way, to data of both sorts which already exist and can be accessed and analysed by others (most notably the data deposited at the University of Essex Data Archive). It is not generally the case that undergraduate students are expected to create and analyse large quantities of primary data, due to the time and financial costs involved. It is more usual that you may instead have to *interpret* data already collected and published. We have dealt with the issue of analysing numerical data in Part I of this text. Indeed, the statistical techniques are the same whether we collect the data ourselves (primary data) or make use of data already interpreted by others (secondary data), although we did point out in Chapter 4 that there may be problems with using data which have already been categorised in a particular way (such as aggregate data in the form of official statistics).

What we shall do in the next two chapters is consider how we might incorporate existing qualitative evidence into our own political research, either by turning it into a quantitative form or by maintaining its qualitative format. To refresh your understanding of the two levels of analysis which we can employ:

> Analysing data that were collected for some other reason or by some other organization is called *secondary analysis*, as contrasted with the *primary analysis* which you carry out on data you collect yourself. Secondary analysis as a form of research is increasingly popular as more and more high-quality data sets covering a very wide range of topics become available.
>
> (Fielding and Gilbert, 2000, pp. 4–5)

Therefore, we subject the data we create ourselves to primary analysis, whilst some data can only be subject to secondary analysis (data sets created by the British Election Studies, polling companies and the OECD, for example). Although these are examples of quantitative data sets, exactly the same principles apply when we analyse qualitative data, as this chapter will demonstrate.

In this chapter, we shall consider some of the most common sources we may use, such as the media and political biographies and autobiographies, and we shall focus upon the *techniques* of analysis. We build upon this in Chapter 8 by extending our analysis to a consideration of official documents and other resources, and draw together our comments with two detailed case studies.

Sources of existing political data

In order to answer a political research question, it may be more appropriate to analyse data which already exist, rather than collect new information. This may be due to time and cost restraints, but also because we need to take account of historical context. Existing data can be located in a variety of formats: databases, the Census, the media, or written or recorded documents in the form of letters, diaries and biographies, for example. Just because data exist, however, does not necessarily mean that we can only carry out secondary analysis. Here, we briefly outline the contribution that some of these sources may make to political research (in the next chapter we shall focus upon official documents and archival data), before moving on in the next section to look at the methods of analysis which might be employed.

Before we progress, however, it is worthwhile clarifying exactly how primary and secondary levels of analysis of existing qualitative data differ. The level of analysis is often decided by the *quality* of the data rather than its *type*. Quality does not imply good or bad as such, but rather the content of the data. Analysis of existing evaluations is secondary analysis (an examination of the political stance of newspaper leaders, for example). Information has already been interpreted by journalists and editors, and we are further assessing this interpretation. If we employ autobiographies to gain a feel for political experiences, we are again conducting secondary analysis (and by their very nature biographies are a form of secondary analysis in themselves).

You may be misled into believing that primary analysis using these sources is not possible, but this would be incorrect. We can, for example, count the number of times a particular story or person appears in newspapers: this is primary analysis (see the example of the work of Glasgow University Media Group (GMUG) below). If we use an autobiography to make an assessment about the political allegiance of the author, this is also primary analysis. Gibson and Ward (2000), for example, employed primary analysis to examine political party internet sites (see below). The difference between primary and secondary sources, therefore, does not necessarily lie in 'what they are' but in 'what we do with them'.

The mass media

A vast amount of political information is presented via media formats, particularly newspapers, television and radio. The most important concern to bear in mind is that it differs from academically generated data in two ways: in terms of its intention and its presentation. Perhaps the dominant concern from an academic perspective centres around the issues of *reliability* and *validity*. Newspapers in particular tend to be politically partisan in the UK, and even the broadcasting media are accused of presenting 'news values' rather than plain facts (Negrine, 1989, p. 4). Thus:

> Although not considered scholarly material, the popular press disseminates much political information. The popular press, which includes magazines, newspapers, and radio and television broadcasts, should be consulted when it is the only source for current information on political players and events; when it can be helpful in identifying the importance of political issues; and when we want to study how the media, which often shape public opinion, report an event.
> (Mannheim and Rich, 1995, p. 53)

Therefore, despite the existence of bias, this does not mean that media sources are of no value in political research, and we need to appreciate that the media are the primary, if not the only, source of political information for many people. They also, of course, have great value in presenting up-to-date political information. When you read an academic book or even a journal article, the reality is that months or even years of work have gone into producing that information and added to this is the actual time it takes for the publishers to bring it out in print. Therefore, media resources can provide a valuable understanding of the *context* of political behaviour, particularly when we might not have direct access to the event we wish to analyse (such as an election campaign in another country). A good place to start when wishing to study newspapers in any detail is the National Newspaper Library at Colindale in London. Hennessy (1988, pp. 19–20) suggests that newspapers are 'strong on personality – who's up and who's down', whilst in contrast they provide a relatively poor guide to the construction of public policy.

Much research has been conducted by the Glasgow University Media Group into the differences between the presentation and interpretation of news stories. Strikes, for example, have been the focus of several studies, and research has shown that the same stories can be interpreted by different people in varying ways. For example, when a report of violent behaviour during the 1984–5 miners' strike was viewed by individuals, some blamed the violence on the miners and others on the police (Philo, 1990, p. 5). As the report was presented to every person in an identical format, existing knowledge and previous experiences must have had some bearing upon interpretation, and as such what is intended in presentation may be very different from how the data are viewed.

As Mannheim and Rich's earlier comment demonstrates, the range of media data is broad, and we might employ different sources, depending upon the particular political question we wish to examine. For example: 'Newspapers are an excellent source of current and historical information including the texts of important speeches, commentaries on political issues, and results of public opinion polls' (Mannheim and Rich, 1995, p. 53).

In contrast, we may turn to television as a resource if we are interested in the agenda; for example, which news stories are run first, to analyse the concentration upon political personalities, or to understand 'imagery': 'television does not represent the manifest actuality of our society, but rather reflects, symbolically, the structure of values and relationships beneath the surface' (Fiske and Hartley, 1996, p. 24).

As Hennessy (1988, p. 25) claims: 'Television is less satisfactory than radio as a medium for deep contemporary history, as the old truism that the need for pictures distorts the message is, well, true.' We should not, therefore, underestimate the contribution that the media can make to political research. They often provide a much more effective source for particular details than poring over books and long articles, and they form a central data source for contemporary issues – particularly if we wish to know more about day-to-day developments in policy making and activities in Parliament or are interested in certain personalities. The proviso, of course, is that we should be aware of biases that may exist.

One area of political research in which the remit of the media has been brought into question is the ability it may have to influence voting behaviour. The dominance of a pro-Conservative press in the 1970s and 1980s in particular led many academics to question the role of the media in 'shaping' political attitudes. Existing research tends to fall between two polar views: those who believe that the media can influence voter choice, and those who adopt a 'selective reinforcement' view; we use particular media stories to support what we already believe.

The role of the media in general election campaigns has been closely monitored in the UK in the post-war period. For example, while newspapers are free to pursue preferred political partisanships, television is subject to strict rules of 'fairness'. Section 93 of the Representation of the People Act (1983) aims to prevent 'any candidate from gaining an unfair advantage over another candidate as a result of getting partial radio or television coverage' (Gaber, 1998, p. 222). That is to say, all candidates in a constituency must approve before a broadcast involving any one of those candidates can be aired. It is not surprising then that broadcast election coverage tends to incorporate senior party members only, as they can speak in their capacity as government ministers or shadow ministers, rather than as ordinary election candidates.

Trying to establish exactly how influential the media are in voting behaviour is not straightforward, as 'the reciprocal and mutually interdependent relationship between the various media and their audiences has made it difficult or impossible to study the impact of the media with any certainty or precision' (Newton, 1992, p. 51). The solution for Norris *et al.* (1999) was in fact to employ five methodological tools in order to understand the impact of political communication during the 1997 General Election campaign. Three consisted of traditional survey-style approaches (analysing trends in opinion polls, and results from the British Election Study cross-sectional and panel surveys – see Chapter 2 for an explanation of these). A fourth approach made use of content analysis to examine news and party messages – a tool examined in more detail in this chapter and the next. A fifth, and more unusual, approach consisted of an experimental study of television news. The latter two methods are important as:

> Cross-sectional surveys can . . . demonstrate an association between media use and political attitudes, but this, by itself, fails to unravel the direction of causality . . . many available measures of media use in past surveys are problematic since they usually fail to capture the complexity of patterns of attention to different sources.
>
> (Norris *et al.*, 1999, p. 49)

That is to say, do people vote for the Labour Party because they regularly read a left-wing paper, or do they read the left-wing paper because it is sympathetic towards their own pro-Labour stance? Do we treat what we read in a newspaper with a 'pinch of salt' as we know that what we are reading has a political bias, whereas we trust what we are told by the televised news because we expect it to be impartial? Therefore, although we might find correlations between media consumption and voting behaviour, we are faced with a chicken and egg scenario. By employing the experimental method we may more accurately understand how opinions change when exposed to particular political messages. This is not a new method: it has been used, for example, to study the impact of war propaganda during the Second World War (ibid., p. 50).

The Sanders and Norris experimental study carried out during the 1997 General Election consisted of 1125 participants selected from the Greater London and south-east areas of England and measured their pre- and post-video attitudes. Participants were informed that they were being tested for selective perception rather than for political attitudes in order to reduce *reactivity* (participants consciously changing their natural behaviour as a response to the study). By showing participants different types of videos, the researchers found that: 'although positive coverage clearly improves a party's image among voters, negative news appears not to damage it' (ibid., p. 138). Likewise, positive (or negative) news about one party does not inflict damage (or benefit) on other parties.

Therefore, the mass media are of use for political research but we must bear in mind that political stories are reported for a reason. Whilst some information is factual, much of what we read, view or hear is not.

Party resources

While we might often choose to look to the media to learn more about what political organisations are saying and doing, this is by no means the only resource available for analysis. Wring (1997, p. 70) distinguishes between what he labels the '*free*' media (coverage by newspapers, television and radio) and the '*paid*' or '*controlled*' media (such as advertisements, posters and Internet sites). Political parties in particular are well practised in the art of 'getting their message across' to the general public:

> Parties attempt to contact voters using a variety of sources, from local leaflets and personal canvassing to advertising on bill-boards and in national news-papers . . . daily press releases and party election broadcasts . . . Manifestos provide the fullest official statement of each party's policy proposals and have been widely used to analyse their position across the left–right political spectrum.
>
> (Norris *et al.*, 1999, p. 44)

Various studies have considered the content of party-created resources. For example, party election broadcasts were analysed as part of the study by Norris *et al.* in order to appreciate the message being conveyed, and these data were compared to evidence from interviews with party managers and campaign strategists (therefore, a process of *triangulation*) (ibid., p. 45). A systematic study of party manifestos has been enhanced by the establishment of the European Consortium of Political Research Manifesto Research Group (MRG). In order to compare ideological change in post-war election manifestos, each sentence of each document has been categorised into a 'relevant policy area' along the lines of fifty-six characteristic criteria (established by the MRG), allowing researchers to employ primary-level quantitative analysis to assess shifts in policy positions. Therefore, while political manifestos are not widely read by the British public:

> Their importance is that they are read by the political and media elite and reported intensively in newspapers, TV and radio. Thus their textual emphases set the tone and themes of campaign discussion. The document does, therefore, represent the way party leaders, after lengthy consideration, want to present themselves to the public.
>
> (Budge, 1999, p. 2)

An analysis of the media's reporting of manifestos would however be classed as secondary analysis.

Biography, autobiography and political memoirs

Political memoirs and autobiographies are personal accounts of political events and experiences, whilst biographies are written by a second person, often through the use of interviews or access to personal papers. Both offer interpretations of politics and are obviously open to a great deal of subjectivity and personal opinion. Diaries, in particular, can overemphasise particular events and misrepresent relationships (Barnes, 1988, p. 41). McRobbie (2000, p. 28) claims that the production of autobiographies has been central to the development of the women's movement: 'Feminists recognise the close links between personal experience and the areas chosen for study – autobiographies invade and inform a great deal of what is written.'

Gamble (1994, p. 35) describes political memoirs as a 'highly accessible source for political scientists', although they may differ in relation to the insight they give us into party political events at the time. A proliferation of memoirs has emerged since the late 1980s (particularly from former Conservative ministers). They also vary in terms of the degree of research they have involved. Barnes (1988) identifies four types of biography: those written with full access to subject's papers; those constructed from public records but with some co-operation; those constructed from press cuttings and the like; and those constructed from interviews. Yet whatever the original source:

> The value of memoirs, however well documented, inevitably diminishes once the historian has access to the relevant source materials. Even then, however, they often retain some value as a guide to sources, and, particularly where there are few if any diaries, they will remain important as the source of a good deal of material which never found its way on to paper, and occasionally some that did but is no longer extant.
>
> (Ibid., p. 36)

If we take the resignation of Margaret Thatcher as Prime Minister in 1990 as an example, we can see that different authors have written about the event from different perspectives. For example, the political journalist John Cole (1995) and the former defence minister Alan Clark (1994) both write about the event in terms of focusing upon who would replace her, whilst Margaret Thatcher herself presents the event in terms of when she decided it was appropriate to resign, and how she informed each minister (Clark's is in fact the only one written in diary format). Therefore, we can see that different authors can report an identical event in qualitatively different ways. Gamble (1994, p. 39) claims that these sources of data can tell us much about ethos and style. In relation to Clark's diaries, we can see that: 'what were crucial events to him receive cursory mention in Thatcher's own memoirs', whilst in contrast, Thatcher's own memoirs are far less personal in style but are far more useful for appreciating the process of policy formation. Briefing box 7.1 highlights some good examples of political autobiographies, biographies and memoirs.

> **Briefing box 7.1 Examples of political autobiographies, biographies and memoirs**
>
> *Jennie Lee: A Life*
> A political biography by Patricia Hollis which covers the life of the former Labour MP and wife of Aneurin Bevan.
>
> *Tony Blair*
> A political biography by John Rentoul covering his life until the 1997 General Election.
>
> *The Unfinished Revolution*
> Memoirs of Philip Gould, adviser to Tony Blair and Labour Party strategist.
>
> *Conflict of Loyalty*
> Autobiography of Geoffrey Howe (Thatcher's longest-serving Cabinet minister) whose resignation speech in 1990 acted as a catalyst for Thatcher's own resignation as Prime Minister.
>
> *As It Seemed to Me*
> Political memoirs of John Cole, long-time journalist and former political editor of the BBC. Covers events from Gaitskell to Thatcher.
>
> *Diaries*
> Alan Clark's diary-style account of his time as Defence Minister, 1983–91.

The Internet

The Internet can be employed at various stages in the research process, but is particularly useful in providing book reviews, on-line journal articles and similar articles, discussion groups, statistics, and online media resources (Day, 1997, p. 184). However, the sheer wealth of data available via the World Wide Web (WWW) can itself make it a problematic research tool. A general search for a particular word or phrase can be time-consuming (and is by no means guaranteed to be productive), and the information you locate can vary tremendously in terms of its quality and relevance. It is perhaps wiser to stick to 'official' web sites for data, particularly if relying upon political parties or media sources.

What we have to bear in mind, of course, is that web sites are created for a purpose. While access to the Internet is growing at a rapid rate, it is still more likely to be used by the middle class, and is often aimed at a younger, rather than elderly, audience: 'Indeed, following the election, the Labour Party claimed that it was keen to develop a strong election web-site, precisely because it was a good communication tool for reaching young people' (Ward and Gibson, 1998, p. 98).

The growth in 'official' Internet sites has inevitably led to academic studies. Despite the fact that only 10 per cent of the electorate had access to Internet information during the 1997 General Election, the political parties chose to engage with this medium, allowing Ward and Gibson (1998, p. 94) to carry out a content analysis of twelve parties' web sites in order to measure size of 'space' devoted to the election and the 'quality' (in terms of targeting, rapid response, substantive content and interactive capabilities) of the web design. A further comparative study was carried out during the 1999 European Parliamentary election. Again, to support their findings, Ward and Gibson's research employed a process of *triangulation* (by also conducting qualitative interviews with the parties' Internet officials).

Gibson and Ward identify three particular reasons why small parties may be attracted to using the Internet as a means of political communication. First, it is cheap to put into operation, in terms of both finance and skills. Second, compared to the traditional media, it is not subject to any third-party editorial control (that is, the party can say exactly what it wants). Third, it provides a means of publicity for those on the political extremes who are often overlooked by the mainstream media. However, while cost is low for small parties, the same is true for the major parties who will inevitably have better resources (if they choose to use them), and creating a 'quality web site' is no guarantee that a sympathetic audience or group of voters will emerge (Gibson and Ward, 2000, p. 172).

In relation to the characteristic of 'space', Ward and Gibson (1998, p. 101) found that two parties did not have any election-specific pages in the 1997 General Election, some parties did and others contained election information within their normal site, leading them to suggest that:

> While the Internet may be allowing minor parties to reduce the advantage that major parties enjoy in terms of exposure, in terms of election coverage and the ability to convey an eye-catching and appealing message, the major parties appear to be outstripping their rivals.

Therefore, whilst minor parties are traditionally disadvantaged by the traditional media, for the moment at least they also appear to be relatively weaker when it comes to generating quality web sites. The study also found that many of the parties were poor at using the Internet as a source to recruit new (particularly young) members. Indeed, rather than being innovative, 'The Internet as a tool of communication was conceived of largely in broadcasting terms appropriate to the traditional electronic media' (ibid., p. 102), therefore reinforcing the trends exhibited by television and the newspapers rather than offering an innovative publicity vehicle.

How do we analyse existing political resources?

We have shown that a vast wealth of data is already out there waiting to be analysed, but what exactly are the methodological tools which we can employ? While the data sources we have covered in this chapter are invariably qualitative in their format (that is, they take the form of a written document, newspaper story, radio or television broadcast or web site), we can in fact employ both quantitative and qualitative methods of assessments. If you remember back to earlier chapters, a quantitative analysis involves counting occurrences, whilst a qualitative analysis places greater emphasis upon context and meaning. The two main approaches we can take are referred to as content analysis and semiotics. We shall now consider the ways in which content analysis can be employed in political research, using real examples of research to illustrate the various strengths and weaknesses of such an approach.

Substantive content analysis

One way in which we can carry out an analysis of existing qualitative data is via *substantive content analysis*. This is basically a systematic literature search which involves identifying key words or phrases (Mannheim and Rich, 1995, p. 41): 'Content analysis provides us with a method – really a set of methods – by which we may summarize fairly rigorously certain direct physical evidences of the behavior of, and the relationships between, various types of political actors' (ibid., pp. 184–185).

This method of research has been greatly advantaged in recent years in two ways. First, the production of CD-ROMs means that we can carry out searches of full-text newspaper articles fairly effortlessly, rather than having to deal with stacks of newspaper back copies (which can be time-consuming, space-consuming and dirty!). However, do not make the mistake of believing that a CD-ROM search will do all the hard work of research for you, as these types of computer searches have two potential limitations: 'First, the search is only as good as the key words we use. Second, the search is only as good as the data base it covers. Either or both of these factors can significantly limit the utility of a computer-generated bibliography' (ibid., p. 47). Therefore, we need to pay close attention to the language which may be used to describe the particular topic we are researching, and consider whether this may differ depending upon the sources we employ. Once we have decided upon which format of communication we are to analyse we can then begin the study.

In relation to television-based research, Fiske and Hartley (1996, p. 21) define substantive content analysis in the following manner:

> It is based upon the non-selective monitoring, usually by a team of researchers, of the total television output for a specified period. It is not concerned with questions of quality, of response or interpretation, but confines itself to the large scale, objective survey of manifest content.'

If we refer back to the Glasgow University Media Group's (GUMG) study of strikes, we can identify clear parameters for analysis. For example, by operational-ising a primary sources analysis, they counted the number of occasions on which a dispute registered by the Department of Employment was reported in 'the media, broadcasting and press' during January and February 1975, but further restricted their study to: 'dispute reports receiving bold type headline or any mention in excess of ½ column inch. Hence, single sentence mentions of disputes "packaged" with other items were not included in this newspaper count' (Eldridge, 1995, p. 143). From this study, the GUMG were able to conclude that news coverage of strikes was 'in a statistical sense at least' unrepresentative of real events and that what in fact was presented as news was 'the skewed nature of industrial reporting' (ibid., p. 164). This reinforces our earlier point that what we are in fact subjected to are 'news values', where some stories and events are prioritised, and others are ignored or overlooked.

For example, 'sleaze' was a substantive story during the 1992–7 government (particularly in the tabloids) yet focused on a small number of individuals. The amount of media coverage may have in fact exaggerated its true extent.

A second quality of existing data which we may choose to take into account when conducting content analysis is the *context* in which words or phrases are provided. For example, we may decide to carry out research which compares attitudes within the tabloid press towards two prime ministers. We may decide to narrow down our study to just two examples, such as John Major and Tony Blair. When conducting our research we may search for three phrases: 'the Prime Minister', 'John Major' and 'Tony Blair'. However, when it comes to analysing our data it may be more useful for us to place references into sub-groups – for example, positive and negative comments. Referring again to the GUMG's study of strikes, they were able to identify a group of words (dispute, strike, action, stoppage) which were all used by the media to denote a similar activity (Eldridge, 1995, p. 204).

Substantive content analysis was employed by Doig *et al.* (1999) in their examination of 'cronyism'. Here, the researchers chose to build upon earlier research into the proliferation of the term 'sleaze' in the national press. Sleaze was a word often linked with the 1992–7 Conservative government and was applied to a range of political activities and events. However:

> Since the 1997 election the term sleaze is still used to describe the failings of the ousted Tory government as well as those of New Labour. Cronyism has, however, become a new word-formula favoured by the media, 'Tony's cronies' having a useful alliterative ring, in seeking to demonise a particular area of concern which is somewhat narrower than the misdemeanours encompassed by the term sleaze.
>
> (Ibid., p. 682)

We can see from this study that the words or phrases we use are crucial to the outcome of our research. For Doig and his colleagues, 'cronyism' is one aspect of sleaze, but it is nevertheless a phrase which has become popular in 'press-speak', partly to differentiate the misdemeanours of the Labour government from the misdemeanours of its predecessor. Rather than just searching for the two words in a selection of the popular press, Doig *et al.* also examined cases where the word 'cronyism' was linked to other terms (such as 'Blair', 'MP', 'minister' and 'Parliament').

The subtleties of context, which may lie undiscovered by substantive content analysis, are demonstrated by an example from the 1997 General Election. The *Daily Mail* was one of the newspapers that retained a pro-Conservative stance, yet despite its attempts via editorials to support the government, it probably did damage to the Conservative Party in other ways, by continually leading with headlines which highlighted the party's scandals and disunity (Norris, 1998, p. 121).

As we mentioned earlier, content analysis was employed by Norris *et al.* (1999) as part of their analysis of the 1997 General Election campaign. One element of their study involved an assessment of 'the favourability of television news during the 1997 campaign' (p. 31). By employing content analysis, Norris *et al.* hoped to answer the questions outlined in Briefing box 7.2. The study covered a variety of newspapers and

> **Briefing 7.2 Research questions examined by content analysis**
>
> - How much news was devoted to each of the main parties?
> - What issues were prioritised?
> - What was the balance of 'positive' and 'negative' messages?
> - How did coverage vary between the news media (that is, newspapers and television)?
> - How did coverage vary during the course of the campaign?
>
> Source: Norris *et al.* (1999, p. 44)

daily news programmes. The 'tone' of each story was rated on a seven-point scale in which '1' represented a negative story and '7' a positive story. By adopting this approach, they concluded 'that overall the vast majority of stories were internally "mixed" or balanced in tone, including positive and negative statements' (p. 31).

Structural content analysis

A second way in which we can employ this research approach is *structural content analysis*: 'here we are less concerned with *what* is said than with *how* it is said . . . we are less concerned with subtleties of meaning than with styles of presentation' (Mannheim and Rich, 1995, pp. 192–193). Rather than counting the number of times a word or phrase appears we instead concentrate upon the amount of space or time given to a topic (such as election stop-watching), substantive differences such as an accompanying photograph or illustration, the size of a news headline, the page placement of a story, or the type of reference (headline story, editorial or letter).

Setting up a content analysis study

Slater (1998) identifies three stages which sound content analysis must undergo. We can see from Briefing box 7.3 that the process of setting up the research is very similar to the process for surveys which we discussed in Chapter 3. Just as with surveys, we shall have a research population and we are unlikely to be able to study the whole population. (Think about television news: how many times do news programmes appear on the five terrestrial channels in one day? what about news bulletins? should we include news-related programmes such as *Newsnight*? how do we go about measuring news on 24-hour channels? There is in fact a large quantity of broadcast news out there.) Similarly, if we are researching an 'ongoing' news story (for example, opinion poll ratings of party popularity) rather than a one-off event (such as the resignation of a party leader) we shall have to identify a distinct time-frame in which our study begins and ends. Therefore, when we identify our sample, it should be subject to the 'same rigours and statistical limits as any survey method: samples must be drawn in such a way as to be both representative and significant, while still small enough to be analysed in depth' (ibid., p. 235).

Briefing box 7.3 Stages of content analysis

- Sampling;
- coding;
- counting.

Source: Slater (1998, pp. 235–236)

Second, we have to decide what to code and how to code it. As we suggested earlier, the final analysis will only be as good as the coded categories employed. As with surveys, similar rules apply to coding; for example, the categories should be exhaustive, mutually exclusive and enlightening. We can take two steps to ensure appropriate categories are employed: (a) we can carry out a pilot study (we might find, for example, the coding for *positive* and *negative* statements alone is not very useful as all the statements are negative – this itself is hardly enlightening); or (b) we may employ a technique of *inter-coder reliability* in which we ascertain whether the same texts hold the same meaning for different people – the higher the degree of consensus, the greater the confidence of reliability (ibid., p. 236). Only then can we progress to stage 3: the counting of those words, phrases and images central to our study.

Disadvantages of content analysis

The main barriers we may confront when attempting to conduct content analysis are summarised in Briefing box 7.4.

Although there is a wealth of documentation and communication to analyse, we should not assume that it is all free or available. Documents provided for public consumption (for example, newspapers and published texts) are not problematic, but some formats (private diaries, internal memoranda) are, and thus we may face similar problems of access as we discussed in relation to observation and interviews in Chapters 6 and 7. Unless documents have been deposited in public access libraries, it is always important to obtain permission before making use of them in research (Mannheim and Rich, 1995, p. 185). Added to this are the ethical considerations to which we must pay attention if the data are of a private or confidential nature (ibid., p. 194).

Briefing box 7.4 Potential problems facing content analysis

- Access;
- sampling;
- criteria;
- context.

Where exactly do we begin or end? As with all other methods of political research, it is important to define a study population. For example, is it feasible to analyse all newspaper coverage of the 1997 General Election? If we are researching an institution (for example, quangos) rather than a specific event we may also need to identify a particular period for assessment. We may also need to limit the population of our source material. Do we wish to analyse all news stories which focus upon the European Union or only those cases in which it makes the lead story? As such, sampling is just as important to research involving existing data as it is to the development of our own surveys and interviews (ibid., p. 186).

Third, if we relate back to the earlier quote made by Mannheim and Rich, you will remember that we claimed that content analysis is only as good as the terms, or words, used. If we conduct a literal search using a computer we shall only find that exact word, rather than those with similar meanings. Referring back to our earlier examples of Prime Ministers, imagine if we searched for the word 'Major'. How many times would this appear in an average news story? We are only interested in the word in relation to a particular person. It is important to spend some time considering whether related words or phrases will fulfil our search requirements: 'references to immigration issues, for example, may be veiled in conciliatory words about political asylum' (ibid., p. 188). One solution to this problem is to undertake a 'piloting' process where we examine a small sample of our research area, and develop 'judgements about the contexts and uses of terms' (ibid., p. 190).

Fourth, we should interpret the document in a way which reflects its purpose. For example, for whom was the document intended? Mannheim and Rich (1995, p. 184) identify three specific classifications of communications. The first includes those internally generated by the individual, organisation or government for internal direction which reflect the decision making process. The second comprises those internally generated but externally directed which might reflect or obscure the decision making process. The third contains those externally generated and internally directed (campaign propaganda). The language used in an internal party memorandum may be very different to a mail-shot aimed at the wider population (ibid., 1995, p. 194).

Those who criticise content analysis tend to do so because of its positivistic approach, and suggest that an alternative approach may be more appropriate if we wish to make sense of cultural influences:

> Content analysis, as an old and rather positivist-inclined method, characteristic of mid-century American sociology, tends to fairly mechanistic readings and conclusions; semiotics, on the other hand, seeks to draw out the full complexity of textual meaning, as well as the act of reading texts, but with little rigour in a conventional sense.
>
> (Slater, 1998, p. 234)

Rather than counting words and phrases, semiotics focuses upon the *interpretation* of documents. This is very much a qualitative research approach and, as such, takes on many of the characteristics of techniques such as ethnography (for example, it produces rich data, but it does not produce generalisable results). Semiotics is most strongly associated with the work of Barthes and Saussure, rather than political scientists:

Semiological analysis proceeds by isolating sets of codes around which the message is constructed . . . These codes constitute the 'rules' by which different meanings are produced and it is the identification and consideration of these in detail that provides the basis to the analysis.

(McRobbie, 2000, p. 77)

That is not to say it does not have a role to play in political research: 'In analysing, say, a news report of a politician being interviewed, we might look at how code of dress, posture and gesture operate to represent the man as presidential or oppositional or whatever' (Slater, 1998, p. 242).

However, this leaves us with a technique which is very open to subjectivity, and which, certainly alone, would be likely to produce controversial data. The more 'scientific' approach exemplified by content analysis allows for replication and comparative studies, and is therefore more likely to be employed.

Case study: the media's portrayal of leadership qualities

As we suggested in our overview of the media, what we are commonly presented with are 'news values' rather than plain facts. This is particularly the case with political leaders. In the post-war period, the party leader has increasingly become the embodiment of his or her political party, and therefore the image that is put across by the media often comes to dominate political news, leading Seymour-Ure (1998, p. 144) to ask: 'have perceptions of leaders' personalities ever been more central to party competition in Britain?'

We have already pointed out that the focus upon senior party personnel can, at least in principle, be blamed upon section 93 of the Representation of the People Act (1983), leading Goddard et al. (1998, p. 164) to suggest that: 'Television's propensity for reporting personality is well known, with the result that leader and personality-focused campaigns seem to be as much an effect of television itself as any other factors.' Indeed, content analysis of the press coverage of political figures during the 1997 campaign demonstrates a heavily masculine, pro-leader emphasis (Norris, 1998, p. 137).

What we shall do here is to present an overview of a selection of the studies which have focused upon leadership portrayal at election time, particularly in relation to newspaper reporting (as we are likely to witness more emotive reporting than is the case with television news). A contrast of the last two general elections is particularly illuminating as the popular press shifted from a predominantly pro-Conservative stance in 1992 to a pro-Labour (or more accurately pro-Blair) stance in 1997. So, how exactly did the media portray the two major party leaders (Major and Kinnock) in 1992, and to what extent had this changed by 1997 (Major and Blair)?

If we look first at the 1992 campaign, Seymour-Ure (1995, p. 140) analysed the imagery portrayed by the Sun and The Mirror newspapers, and demonstrates that the Sun tended to employ negative imagery of Kinnock rather than of the Labour Party in general. In contrast, television was 'highly leader-orientated', including coverage of the leaders' wives (Nossiter et al., 1995, p. 90). The coding of television coverage by Nossiter et al. found that coverage tended to be descriptive rather than evaluative, but that there was a difference between stations, with ITV being more evaluative than the BBC (ibid., p. 35).

In relation to the 1997 General Election campaign, the newspapers' attack on the Conservative Party was no more than a continuation of a decline in support which began with the events of Black Wednesday (16 September 1992). Negative language was continually used to portray John Major in the tabloids: phrases such as 'damaged goods' in the *Sun* (Norris, 1998, pp. 118–119); and 'political pygmy', 'leadership of a lizard' and 'status of a performing flea' in the *Mirror* (Seymour-Ure, 1997, p. 78).

In terms of methodology, Seymour-Ure concentrated upon newspaper portrayal of Major and Blair, focusing on the content of editorials and leading articles only. He assessed characterisation of the two party leaders by considering whether both personality and professional skills were portrayed in a positive or negative way, and with which policies or topics the leaders were linked. Examples of positive personal characteristics were 'tough, combative, courageous' and 'man of the people' whilst negative characteristics were 'weak, panicking, cowardly' and 'arrogant, smug, vain and power-hungry'. Similarly, professional skills were 'experienced' and 'effective', whilst the negative ones were 'inexperienced' and 'ineffective, dismal' (Seymour-Ure, 1998, p. 134).

Seymour-Ure (ibid., p. 133) recognises that some of the overall impact of characterisation can be lost when content analysis is used to classify text: 'The pungency of newspaper prose is lost in this process. For example, the statement that "John Major couldn't run a bath" is coded blandly under "incompetent".' By employing content analysis, Seymour-Ure was able to show that the pro-Labour papers were uncritical of Blair but highly critical of Major, whilst pro-Conservative papers were critical of Blair but unable to praise Major's positive qualities. In addition, the *Mirror* changed its language: having portrayed Major as boring and ineffective in 1992, by 1997 it portrayed him as arrogant, indecisive and incompetent (ibid., pp. 136–144).

In contrast, Scammell and Harrop's (1997) analysis focused upon an alternative imagery: press photos of the leading party politicians. Here, they found that the Conservative Party was represented in a range of ways – photos of various Eurosceptics, pictures of Major and his wife, Neil Hamilton (thereby highlighting the sleaze factor) and even pictures of Thatcher (making it backward-looking). In contrast, pictures associated with the Labour Party were usually of Tony Blair and his wife, John Prescott and Gordon Brown, leading Scammell and Harrop (ibid., p. 181) to claim that: 'Labour's discipline and the presidential style of contest was reflected in the press pictures.'

Therefore, we can see that the portrayal of political party leaders by the mass media is an accessible topic for researching via content analysis. If we wish to count personality evaluations, we are more likely to employ newspapers as a resource because they tend to be more opinionated (particularly if we make use of tabloid newspapers). In contrast, television is more likely to focus upon senior party personnel than upon ordinary candidates. Rather than measure emotive language, we are more likely to employ this resource to assess the contextual environment, mannerisms and behaviour.

Conclusion

In this chapter we have introduced and evaluated the techniques which we can employ when seeking to integrate existing qualitative data into our own political research. Due to financial and time-related constraints we may find it beneficial to make use of data already produced by others, rather than create 'new' databases of our own.

We have drawn attention to the fact that there are a great deal of existing sources which we can employ in our own political research, such as the mass media, party resources, the Internet, and political autobiographies, biographies and memoirs. Each source is, to a considerable extent, a subjective form of political information, and we identified some of the considerations of which we need to be aware before using any particular source for research purposes.

We have also considered the various methods we can employ to analyse existing political data, by focusing upon a variety of existing studies but also by paying closer attention to the research process known as content analysis (which can be conducted via a substantive or structural approach). We have, furthermore, drawn upon some of the limitations of this method. The important factor to remember is that we need to be just as rigorous if our research employs existing qualitative data as we are when creating our own primary data (via surveys and interviews). We shall expand upon this approach in the next chapter by focusing upon the integration of historical and archival data into political research.

Further reading

For a good introduction to the subject of using documents in research, see R. Finnegan, 'Using Documents', in R. Sapsford and V. Jupp (eds), *Data Collection and Analysis*, London: Sage, 1996 (the eight 'questions to ask' on pp. 146–149 are useful).

For a clear, concise justification of the strengths and weaknesses of particular research tools for studying political campaigns, see P. Norris, J. Curtice, D. Sanders, M. Scammell and H.A. Semetko, *On Message*, London: Sage, ch. 3. A useful example of research involving the Internet can be found in R. Gibson and S. Ward 'An Outsider's Medium? The European Elections and UK Party Competition on the Internet', in P. Cowley, D. Denver, A. Russell and L. Harrison (eds), *The British Elections and Parties Review*, volume 10, London: Frank Cass, 2000.

For an explanation of the use and results of content analysis carried out on newspapers and television during election campaigns see H. Semetko, M. Scammell and T.J. Nossiter, 'The Media's Coverage of the Campaign', in A. Heath, R. Jowell and J. Curtice (eds), *Labour's Last Chance?*, Aldershot: Dartmouth, 1994; C. Seymour-Ure, 'Leaders and Leading Articles: Characterisation of John Major and Tony Blair in the Editorials of the National Daily Press', in I. Crewe, B. Gosschalk and J. Bartle (eds), *Political Communications: Why Labour Won the General Election of 1997*, London: Frank Cass, 1998; M. Scammell and M. Harrop, 'The Press' in D. Butler and D. Kavanagh (eds), *The British General Election of 1997*, Basingstoke: Macmillan, 1997; and C. Seymour-Ure, 'Newspapers: Editorial Opinion in the National Press', in P. Norris and N. Gavin (eds), *Britain Votes 1997*, Oxford: Oxford University Press, 1997.

For an explanation of the use of experimental methods, see D. Sanders and P. Norris, 'Does Negative News Matter? The Effect of Television News in Party Images in the 1997 British General Election', in D. Denver *et al.* (eds), *The British Election and Parties Review*, volume 8, London: Frank Cass.

Chapter 8

Employing historical and archival resources in political research

Lisa Harrison and Jane Martin

Introduction

In the previous chapter we began to consider how and when we might use existing documentation and similar resources (such as television and the Internet) within political research. The advantage is that the material is already in existence, we do not need to construct a survey or interview political actors. However, that does not imply that research using such resources is 'easy' or 'quick' – we are still faced with issues such as sampling, access and even piloting our research. You may have observed that we employed some relatively recent examples of research in Chapter 7 to show how content analysis and other research techniques can be utilised in political science. Yet the resources available are much broader, and May (1997, p. 157) suggests that documents are often undervalued and regarded as crude empiricism when, in fact, 'They can tell us a great deal about the way in which events were constructed at the time, the reasons employed, as well as providing materials upon which to base further research investigations.'

In this chapter we focus on research using existing documentation, but that which is much more historical in context. More precisely, we consider the resources which may be available for political research, and the requirements and process of analysing historical material. We finish by looking at a detailed case study of research that has made use of archival materials.

What do historical and archival resources have to offer political science?

It is important that we are aware of both the strengths and the limitations of documentary sources, and we shall begin with some words of caution. Any research involving historical material is likely to be overshadowed by two concerns: objectivity and lack of first-hand experience. In reality, our understanding of political history is informed by a selective reading of documents. It is highly unlikely, particularly for undergraduate students, that you will have had the time or opportunity to read *everything* about a person (for example, Winston Churchill) or an event (for example, the Vietnam War). Similarly, the *types* of document we read vary in terms of information and accuracy: some are very opinionated or subjective (such as autobiographies, which we discussed in Chapter 7) whilst others may be highly factual and descriptive (such as a government memo). It is important, therefore, that we should not treat documents as neutral sources: 'What people decide to record is itself informed by decisions which, in turn, relate to the social, political and economic environments of which they are a part' (May, 1997, p. 164).

Documents are selective in terms of the information presented. This is usually based upon the requirement of the document when it is initially produced (as we shall see below when we discuss administrative records), but it may also be the case that the author has intentionally decided to record some items and leave others out. Furthermore, documents may be influenced by the social and political environment in which they are produced (a diary written by a defence minister during a conflict may be very different in tone and content to an account written some time after the event). It has been suggested, for example, that documentation has consistently marginalised the role of women in history. Miles (1989) is one of many who argue that history has been written in a way which concentrates upon male, rather than female, achievements (see the case study in this chapter of Mrs Bridges Adams). Of course, some documents are produced with research in mind; others are produced for personal use. It is important to question the sense of social context of production and to whom the document is intentionally addressed.

A second potential disadvantage of employing documentary analysis is that it is similar to observational research in terms of being 'non-reactive'. There is little, if any, opportunity for interaction between the investigator and the subject being studied – we cannot 'travel back in time' to experience an event. It may be possible to converse with a person involved at that time, but this will inevitably be constrained by issues such as location, access and time difference (a 'problem' which we can perceive in the research of Vickers and in our case study). However, despite these two constraints, documentary sources are potentially very broad and detailed. In Briefing box 8.1 we outline some common sources.

Therefore, we can see that documentary material varies significantly in terms of its format, its accessibility and its intended audience. The distinction between formats is important for several reasons. First, it may influence what we may refer to as the document's *authenticity*, or validity. First-hand material has obvious appeal but may be highly opinionated. Second, the format may also affect the level of detail. While tertiary sources are very good 'pointers', they usually lack the detail and context which personal accounts can provide. Thus, classification types have their own advantages and disadvantages. We shall now examine these distinctive classifications in more detail and draw upon relevant examples of documentary research in political science.

Finnegan (1996, p. 141) provides a useful definition of the distinction between primary and secondary sources:

> Primary sources . . . form the basic and original material for providing the researcher's raw evidence. Secondary sources, by contrast, are those that discuss the period studied but are brought into being at some time after it, or otherwise somewhat removed from the actual events. Secondary sources copy, interpret or judge material to be found in primary sources.

To recall the comments made in Chapter 7, primary analysis is an interpretation of raw materials, whereas secondary analysis involves an examination of the interpretations of others. It is possible, therefore, for some sources of documentation to act as both primary and secondary sources, depending upon the exact context of the information we are interested in. As a consequence, secondary documents enable us to learn about a person or event through the experiences of others rather than because we were actually there. Obviously, analysis of a political event (such as the implementation of the 1832 Reform Act) does not necessarily end just because no one with direct experience is still alive. In contrast, secondary sources often lack the same immediacy, although this does not undermine their ability to inform and enlighten.

A useful source of secondary data for political research takes the form of administrative records, as a vast range of data has been collated and recorded

Briefing box 8.1 The dimensions of documentary research

Types of material

1 Historical documents
   • laws, declarations, statutes
2 Government records
   • official statistics, Hansard, ministerial records, debates, political speeches, and committee records
3 Mass media
4 Personal sources
   • biographies, autobiographies and diaries (see Chapter 7)
5 Tertiary sources
   • enable the location of other references, for example, indexes, abstracts and bibliographies

Public vs private material

1 Closed access
   • such as government documents covered by the Official Secrets Act
2 Restricted access
   • an example being British Royal papers which are only accessible by the monarch
3 Open-archival
   • documents held at the Public Records Office, the American Library of Congress
4 Open-published
   • examples include Acts of Parliament, Hansard

Solicited vs unsolicited material
The distinction between material produced for general public consumption, and that produced primarily for private consumption.

Source: May (1997, pp. 159–162)

by organisations and individuals, and the increase in computerised records is expanding the opportunities for their use in research. However, as they are created for administrative purposes, they may not hold all the data we would find most useful, and so:

> The design of records-based studies has to be back to front. Instead of designing the study, and then collecting the necessary data, one obtains details of the contents and characteristics of a set of records and then identifies the corresponding research model.
>
> (Hakim, 1993, p. 133)

Administrative records can, for example, be useful in analysing organisational policy and decision making processes (such as patterns of recruitment and promotion within an organisation). As Hakim (ibid.) suggests, such records can also provide 'a key source of data on events or groups too small and scattered or otherwise difficult to trace for national interview surveys to be a realistic possibility'. While we should not underestimate the usefulness of administrative sources for political research, we should be careful about maintaining the confidentiality of private records. We have discussed in Chapter 6 the importance of protecting the identity of those we study, and the same applies to some aspects of documentary analysis.

We have already considered personal sources to some extent in Chapter 7, such as diaries and memoirs. One potential problem we may face when researching personal sources is that it is often the case that private papers are not published in a single volume. Therefore, probably the most challenging aspect we may face when conducting research using historical documents is their location (see the case study of Mrs Bridges Adams below). One issue which may determine the outcome of any research employing personal sources is our awareness of the breadth of documentation.

It is not surprising that many political researchers decide, at some point, to engage with archival research. We have already made reference to the University of Essex Data Archive, but the term 'archive' usually has a more mainstream meaning, and is defined by Cox (1988, p. 71) as consisting of:

> the papers (or, usually, a selection from the papers) which official authorities (in the case of the archives of the state, the central government) drew up for the purposes of the conduct of their affairs, or which they used in conducting them. They are papers which themselves *formed an actual part of that conduct of affairs*.
>
> (Italics in original)

Archives are gradually becoming better organised and more accessible (see a list of useful archives in Chapter 10). Nevertheless, we should appreciate that not every document will make its way into an archive, and 'unrecorded' events (such as telephone calls) are lost forever (ibid., p. 82). Do not assume that archives will be as easy to use as a general library; it is worthwhile spending some time planning ahead by checking opening times and the kind of access granted to materials held (Raspin, 1988, p. 96).

It is necessary to appreciate that, just because the government or its agencies produce a document, this does not necessarily make it 'a public document'. All government documents are subject to the 1958 Public Records Act, which means that many are restricted by a 30-year rule, which prohibits public access. If you look at the first edition of a broadsheet newspaper on the first day of the year, you will invariably see reference to formerly protected government memos. However, there are exceptions which go beyond the 30-year rule which apply to

> exceptionally sensitive papers whose disclosure would be contrary to the public interest, on security or other grounds; for records whose release would or might constitute a breach of an undertaking of confidentiality; and for records

whose disclosure would cause distress or danger to living individuals or their immediate descendants.

(Cox, 1988, pp. 79–80)

A classic example is government papers relating to the abdication of Edward VIII, some of which are still inaccessible.

Vickers's (1995) research on the impact of the Cold War upon the international trade union movement relied heavily upon access to archival materials (such as those held at the Trades Union Congress, the Modern Records Centre at Warwick, the National Museum of Labour History at Manchester, the Public Records Office, and the International Institute of Social History based in Amsterdam). The research combined evidence from historical documents with semi-structured interviews conducted with academics, researchers and 'trade unionists who were either active in the early post-war period or had considerable knowledge of it' (p. 168), although this latter group proved to be most problematic because they were difficult to track down or were no longer alive.

Locating an archive which is relevant to our research topic does not necessarily guarantee that the remainder of the research process will run smoothly or be problem-free. Once we have taken access times into account, archival searching can be extremely time-consuming. In terms of the 'usefulness' of archives, Vickers admits (ibid., p. 172) that:

> The amount of information I gathered from the archives varied. Sometimes I would use files that were a goldmine of information, and sometimes I would spend what seemed an eternity working through files that turned out to have nothing much of interest. This, I have since realised, is typical of archival analysis.

A common obstacle to archival work is that information we might 'expect' to find is unlocatable (possibly because it does not exist!). You must also bear in mind that different institutions have different rules about consulting and copying documents (do not expect to be able to photocopy documents). There is always the problem of 'representativeness', as archival material is only as good as the content of the archive:

> The main limitation of such data is the tendency to produce 'top-down' studies (skewed by the thoughts of elites) . . . in my experience, archival analysis alone cannot bridge the gulf and must therefore be supplemented wherever possible with oral histories and interview techniques.

(Ibid., p. 176)

Therefore, whilst archives are a potentially extremely useful source of material for documentary research, be prepared for frustrations and disappointments. While all expectations may not be met, it is also possible that unexpected issues and accounts may be discovered. As with Hakim's (1993) comments on research employing administrative records, be prepared for your research question to be guided by the material available, rather than establishing an experimental hypothesis approach.

There are some excellent sources of tertiary information in political science. For example, sources of factual information include *Keesing's Contemporary Archives*, *Dod's Parliamentary Companion* and *The Civil Service Yearbook*. In addition, political researchers often make use of Butler and Butler's *British Political Facts* (1994), F.W.S. Craig's *British Parliamentary Election Results*, and Waller and Criddle's *Almanac of British Politics* (Barnes, 1988, pp. 31–32). A good politics library should contain most, if not all, of these.

Inevitably, much political research of a historical nature will rely upon a combination of sources or data types. McLean and Bustani's (1999) study of the 1846 Repeal of the Corn Laws combined evidence from the Aydelotte data set on roll call in the Parliament of 1841–7, Hansard, the 1851 Census, and information gleaned from Sir Robert Peel's memoirs and Gladstone's diaries. The researchers also made use of the Wellington Papers (located at the University of Southampton). The Aydelotte data set is what we would refer to as secondary data as it was 'augmented from primary sources, and the letters and memoranda of the principal actors' (McLean and Bustani, 1999, p. 817) but combined this with information from administrative records such as schooling, club membership, relationship to aristocracy, business interests, military service, and wealth at death (ibid., p. 827). Combining these varied, yet informative, sources of historical data led McLean and Bustani to conclude that: 'none of the standard explanations of Repeal works well' (p. 834), but that Peel and Wellington were central to the abolition of agricultural protection even though both Houses of Parliament were dominated by landed interests.

The requirements and process of documentary analysis

So far, we have considered some of the many and varied sources of documentation which may enable us to conduct worthwhile political research. Now we shall concentrate upon how we might operationalise this research approach. Vickers (1995, p. 175) stresses the centrality of having a research aim, or hypothesis, when conducting historical research:

> A fact that many students fail to realize is that historical research usually requires the setting up of specific, testable hypotheses. Without such hypotheses, historical research often becomes little more than an aimless gathering of facts.
>
> (1995, p. 175 taken from Borg, 1963, pp. 189–190)

The origins of documentary analysis in social science can be traced back to the early twentieth century (Jupp and Norris, 1993), and it was a method particularly favoured by the Chicago School of Sociology (exemplified in the work of Thomas and Znaniecki and their life-history research on Polish immigrants). Jupp and Norris claim that since then documentary research has developed via three dominant paradigms. The first of these, content analysis, represents a positivist paradigm which dominated social science in the 1960s (and, as we have shown in Chapter 7, it is still frequently used in combination with other methods in political science). Lasswell, for example, adopted a positivist approach in 1942 when looking at the terminology of war propaganda. Since then, we have also seen the emergence (particularly in sociological studies) of interpretivism and discourse analysis. Rather than counting the occurrence of words and phrases, or comparing the use of contextual mechanisms such as headlines or imagery, supporters of these two paradigms argue that documentary research requires more than just descriptive analysis. Rather:

> Critical analysis in social science involves an examination of the assumptions that underpin any account (say, in a document) and a consideration of what other possible aspects are concealed or ruled out. It can also involve moving beyond the documents themselves to encompass a critical analysis of the institutional and social structures within which such documents are produced.
>
> (Jupp, 1996, p. 298)

The two approaches do differ. For the interpretivists, documents should be analysed in terms of the social constructions they contain (Jupp and Norris, 1993, p. 43). If we refer back to the study by Doig *et al.* (1999) outlined in Chapter 7, we saw that the terms 'sleaze' and 'cronyism' have been employed by the national press to refer to similar forms of political actions. However, while cronyism refers to a narrower range of misdemeanours, an important difference is that sleaze is associated with one type of government (under the Conservatives) and cronyism another (led by Labour).

In contrast, discourse analysts believe that documents are a medium through which power is expressed. Of particular interest to discourse analysis is the use of language in defence relations, for example, the construction of terms such as 'war' and 'peace'. Discourse analysis is primarily, but not solely, associated with the work of Foucault. Foucault argued that documents are not of interest because of what they tell us about the author, but because they inform us about the mechanisms through which power is exercised (Jupp and Norris, 1993, p. 49). While we shall not explore the minutiae of these two approaches here, it is important to recognise that 'One consequence has been a blurring of the once important division between, on the one hand, an objective, value-neutral, empirical social science, and, on the other, those approaches stressing interpretative and essentially evaluative methods of inquiry' (Howarth, 1998, p. 268).

In adopting an interpretivist or discourse analysis approach, one would believe that the critical analysis of a document involves much more than carrying out the sorts of content analysis we referred to in Chapter 7, rather questioning why the document was produced, what is being said (overtly and covertly) and what is not being said. Furthermore, we need to be aware of the particular language used (and the meaning that lies behind it) and of the social relations that inform the different stages of history (Jupp and Norris, 1993, p. 47). Remember that when we looked at the work of Vickers, it was suggested that archives tend to present an elitist view of events, because 'important' people are more likely to have chronicled their lives and left their papers behind. Furthermore, these accounts tend to be male-dominated. As such, there are certain issues, which we need to consider when undertaking documentary research that we have identified in Briefing box 8.2.

When we decide to use documentary evidence in political research, we make

> **Briefing box 8.2 Potential challenges to documentary research**
>
> - *Authenticity* – soundness and authorship;
> - *credibility* – similarity and accuracy;
> - *representativeness* – survival and availability;
> - *meaning* – literal and interpretative understanding.
>
> Source: Scott (1990, p. 6)

assumptions about the quality of the document. We hope that the document is 'genuine', or what is termed *authentic*, although it is possible for its authenticity to be challenged in several ways. First, it may lack authenticity because it contains inconsistent errors. Imagine, for example, that a document claims that '*Minister X resigned on 30 February 2000*'. This is logically incorrect, as February never has more than twenty-nine days. Of course, this may be a single overlooked error, but once we find such mistakes we have a tendency to question the accuracy of the rest of the document. The soundness of a document may also be challenged when different versions of the same document exist (if two different documents pertain to be the same thing); or the authenticity of a document can be challenged when it is inconsistent in relation to other similar documents (for example, if several government memos identify *Minister X* as making a decision, whilst another memo identifies *Minister Y*). Of course, we do have to allow for some difference in accordance with personal experience. Authenticity may also be challenged in terms of the 'ownership' of a document. It is not always the case that the identity of the author is apparent, and this may be further complicated in terms of political research as: 'A memorandum signed by a government minister, for example, may actually have been produced by one or more of the civil servants responsible for handling ministerial correspondence' (Scott, 1990, p. 21).

Perhaps the best-known case of 'unsound' documentation was the Hitler Diaries. In the early 1980s, various British and German newspapers claimed that the personal diaries of Hitler had been uncovered, and this was verified by a prominent British historian. However, chemical tests on the ink and paper showed them to be forgeries (ibid., pp. 175–176).

A second case of authenticity has centred on the infamous Zinoviev Letter. Zinoviev was the President of the Third Communist International (Comintern) and in this capacity allegedly sent a letter to the British Communist Party, calling for agitation among troops and munitions workers to mobilise against an alleged Anglo-Soviet trade treaty. The letter was published four days before the General Election in 1924, creating a 'red scare' which some held responsible for the electoral defeat of the first Labour government. The letter had been denounced as a fake at the time by some (the *Daily Herald* and Russian authorities), but when the case was reopened in 1967 by *The Sunday Times*, a forgery theory was proposed. In 1997, previously private documents were released, leading Gill Bennett to conclude that the letter was a forgery which had been created on behalf of members of the British secret services to benefit the Conservative Party (*Guardian*, February 1999). The case shows that the issue of authenticity is a particular problem when investigating events involving 'secret' information.

A second challenge we face when using historical documents is *credibility*. Is the document we are analysing reliable? Credibility 'refers to the extent to which the evidence is undistorted and sincere, free from error and evasion' (Scott, 1990, p. 7). For a document to be credible, we need to be aware of the purpose of the document. Was it produced to describe events, to persuade (such as a political party leaflet), or to self-protect (such as a ministerial memo)? 'The purpose of a communication, then can provide an important context for understanding its content, and we must attempt, when possible, to ferret out this information' (Mannheim and Rich, 1995, p. 194). We would not, for example, expect a newspaper to report a parliamentary debate in exactly the same way as Hansard – we would expect the newspaper to be more opinionated. This is not to imply that you should be suspicious of every document you encounter. Indeed, the majority of documents cover very mundane and uncontentious issues. Yet there is always a possibility, particularly with personal letters, diaries and other such documents that these provide a means for expressing very personal feelings:

> The question of 'sincerity', therefore, is the question of whether the author of the document actually believed what he or she recorded . . . personal documents may be produced for a whole variety of reasons ranging from self-justification to exhibitionism to the intellectual search for the meaning of life.
>
> (Scott, 1990, p. 22)

Third, we need to ask whether the document is *representative* – and this centres around the idea of 'typicality' (May, 1997, p. 170). Are we looking at a unique view or does it represent a 'general mood of the time'? This is not, however, to suggest that non-typical documents do not in themselves have any research use. Representativeness is an issue to which we should pay particular attention when using archives, and Scott (1990, pp. 7–8) suggests, we should ask 'whether the archivists or clerks responsible for storing the schedules have used additional selection or sampling methods to reduce the bulk of the material to be stored'.

Finally, we need to pay attention to the *meaning* of the document. Is the document clear and comprehensible? Has the meaning of language changed? What was the distribution remit of the document? For example, different types of newspapers are written with different audiences in mind (Mannheim and Rich, 1995, p. 194). A potential problem with personal papers (particularly diaries) is that the author may have used codes and abbreviations that we are unable to translate accurately (May, 1997, p. 167).

These are important questions to ask about all documentary sources that we might employ in our research. This does not mean that only error-free, typical documents which have a common interpretation can be employed, but that we must be at least aware of any challenges to reliability that might exist, or that others may interpret the information held within differently. What a person records is informed by decisions which relate to their social, political and economic environments, and what is left out may be of more interest than what is actually included. Documents are constructed within a particular social reality.

Case study: Mary Bridges Adams, a life for Labour and education

The background to the research

The trials, tribulations and benefits of conducting historical political research can be understood by considering the on-going biographical project on Mary Bridges Adams (née Daltry, 1855–1939). From the 1890s Bridges Adams played an active public role in one of Britain's leading socialist organisations, even though women did not obtain the vote in general elections until 1918. Researchers have so far only succeeded in building up a partial picture of women's participation in British socialism before suffrage was achieved, and the focus of this particular research project sought to redress some of this imbalance. Her story is of interest, not only for political reasons, but because it elucidates the much-overlooked contribution that women have made to Labour movement history. Such an assessment has its difficulties but this case outlines the reasons why a study of Mary Bridges Adams is important.

The research 'problem'

Turning to the past means much more than focusing solely upon bureaucrats and politicians who wielded enormous influence in the official central state. It can also involve detective work into those places where British women were most influential in the late nineteenth century: in the caring sphere of social politics and activity at the local level. Mary Bridges Adams was excluded from high politics from the whole of her career but she did not wilfully hide herself from history. In her lifetime she preserved a myriad of press cuttings about her activism and objected to her coverage (or lack of it) in the media. Unlike most of the papers of Margaret MacDonald (first President of the Women's Labour League), which were burnt by her husband on her death, we do not know what happened to these. In the intervening years Mary has remained obscure and the attention paid to her by historians has been negligible. Her story is less well known for a number of reasons. On the one hand, attention to women activists has been slow to develop. On the other, there is the scanty nature of the source material, which may explain why papers relating to Mary Bridges Adams have not been collected or referenced together. She does have an entry in the *Dictionary of Labour Biography* but this has not secured her a presence in the story of British socialism. Therefore, a would-be biographer has to mine for sources. My objective is to produce a many-layered study of one woman: to explore what it meant to be a 'socialist woman' and the ways in which local politics served as leverage for female involvement in public affairs.

Initiating the process of researching the past: the importance of archives

The *Dictionary of Labour Biography* entry for Mary concentrates on her activism during the period from 1900 to 1920 and provides details of where to find out about her life and work. Much of her political activity involved educational administration at local government level, and administrative records were useful in finding out about her contribution as an

133

elected member of the London School Board. Local government provided early opportunities for female politicians in the late nineteenth century; in particular the newly founded school boards established after the 1870 Education Act. Twenty-nine women in London served on the school board between 1870 and its abolition under the 1903 London Education Act. One of them was Mary, who served from 1897 to 1904. In due course, the starting point for this research was a consultation of the files held at the London Metropolitan Record Office, in order to find out more about the institutional papers of the London School Board. Here, I was able to locate the School Board *Minutes*, which contain a wealth of informative detail, such as data on attendance at meetings, voting records and motions of policy. In addition, I was able to access sub-committee records and records from individual schools under the control of the board (including those for which Mary became school manager). Background information on the London School Board was also gleaned from the annual report and address of the chairman. The *School Board Chronicle* proved crucial to the study because it offered a blow-by-blow account of debate within the School Board. The rhetorical skills of this female politician were very evident in her speeches even if she did not always influence educational policy making in the city. Always in a minority both as a woman and a socialist, her main concerns were for the extension of educational opportunities, as well as child welfare programmes and policies in London. In part, her work was reported because she was not afraid to say controversial things. This was vital because it ensured that she got noticed even if the attendant publicity offered mixed rewards since the media coverage was often negative.

Widening the search: uncovering public and private resources and some practical considerations

These scattered records obviously present problems. For instance, conventional historical sources would include the documents left by organisations such as the Independent Labour Party and the Social Democratic Federation – annual reports, pamphlets, journals, minute books. However, Mary Bridges Adams did not hold national or local office in her party, the Social Democratic Federation, and she was not a conference delegate. This study offers a challenge to the ready and confident acceptance that the lack of records proves there were no women activists.

Biographical approaches and network analyses form the basis of an attempt at bringing the thoughts of lesser-known figures like Mary Bridges Adams more clearly into focus. This means venturing into specific local investigations in order to find out more about the experiences that influenced her work and the network of significant relationships that made it easier for her to move out of family into public life. Although it is a vast source of research data, local and regional newspapers are one of the best sources of information on women's political involvement in their localities. In London, the press devoted column inches to School Board elections, with space dedicated to the publication of manifestos and very full coverage of speeches and meetings, while letters to the editor could also shed light on political opinion at the time. Sometimes there was biographical information on the candidates: a useful source for women who are less well known today. For instance, the *Illustrated London News* carried a feature on the women contesting the 1897 election, which referred to Mary's father having held an appointment at the Elswick Works, Newcastle, and her beginnings as a pupil teacher. This made it possible to trace the Daltry family in the

1871 Census returns. The census schedules may be consulted in the Public Record Office, London, but local returns are normally available (on microfilm or in transcript) in local record offices and sometimes in large libraries. So, the Tyne and Wear Archives Service found the Daltry family living at the Robin Adair public house, along with the ages of her father and mother, where they were born and their occupation. The returns also showed that she had an elder brother, Thomas, who was a draughtsman. The 15-year-old Mary was listed as a pupil-teacher. It is to be hoped that tracing will eventually make it possible for oral interviews (with descendants) to supplement the historical and archival resources. Along with local newspapers, it is sometimes worth consulting *The Times* index for more detail on individuals, particularly the coverage of high profile events or through the obituaries, which are useful biographical tools. Journals produced by women's groups (like the *Englishwoman's Review*) also contain a range of material to help the researcher discover the part played by women in local government.

It will be recalled that coverage in the *School Board Chronicle* made it possible to assess Mary's performance and analyse her contribution to debate. Her debating profile reveals that she spoke more than the average male member and her contributions tended to be concentrated on child welfare programmes (including the provision of free school meals and medical inspection). The statistics based on columns in the *School Board Chronicle* were supplemented by reports in local newspapers such as the *Kentish Mail* and the *Greenwich and Deptford Observer*. Mary represented Greenwich for seven years and was returned with the support of the Royal Arsenal Co-operative Society, the largest of its kind in Greater London. Information about the Society's association with Mary can be found in the Half-Yearly Reports and the bulletin of the Society, known as *Comradeship*. Like many other working-class women, Mary joined the local branch of the Women's Co-operative Guild which was active in community politics, poor law administration and local authorities. A schoolteacher with a growing reputation as an orator for the labour movement, the key to her electoral success was her trade union and political involvement.

Although it is time-consuming, *prosopography* (collective biography) is a useful methodological tool for investigating the source of political action. The objective is to uncover the common background characteristics of a political group. With this in mind, the National Register of Archives provides a straightforward way of tracking down private papers, but the women who served on the London School Board have left relatively few papers, and their memoirs often paper over the problems they encountered in local government. There are exceptions. There is the unpublished autobiographical fragment written by Florence Fenwick Miller that found its way into the Contemporary Medical Archives Centre at the Wellcome Institute for the History of Medicine. There are also the collections of papers left by Emily Davies, founder of Girton College, Cambridge (deposited in the College archives); and by Helen Taylor, the stepdaughter of John Stuart Mill (deposited in the London School of Economics); as well as the letters of the pioneer doctor Elizabeth Garrett Anderson (in the Fawcett Library, London Guildhall University). All four served in the 1870s and 1880s and were involved in the suffrage movement. Short biographies of their female colleagues were built up almost entirely from secondary sources such as the School Board for London papers, press reports and the documents left by the Women's Local Government Society available at the London Metropolitan Record Office. Today, it is possible to draw on a wider set of sources using search engines on the Internet, which may serve as timesaving devices for historical and biographical political research.

Building up the political profile

In relation to my own research on the female members of the London School Board, the evidence I collated highlighted that these were mostly middle-class women who had leisure, confidence and connections. They had common background characteristics, but there were differences. A few engaged in working-class and labour campaigns and struggles, although the majority did not. Of those who *did*, Mary Bridges Adams stood apart from the rest. First, she was distinctive as the only female member to grow up in a working-class community, and thus lacked the independence of a large unearned income. Second, her story does not show the overlapping membership of women's organisations of Liberal party affiliation evident in the biographies of most London School Board women. Third, she was exceptional in seeking election while the mother of a young child. Among a group of elite and privileged women, who were themselves 'different' from the majority of women, she stood out as an example of independence. These aspects interested and intrigued me.

By 1901, Mary Bridges Adams helped to organise trade union opposition to the proposed abolition of the school board system after the accession to power of a strong Conservative government. It could be argued that she was ahead of her time since she opposed the educational provision based on overt social class divisions that continued to be a dominant feature of English education. More immediately, the abolition of the London School Board by the 1903 London Education Act was a watershed for female politicians, since it disenfranchised women as voters, political candidates and elected representatives. Although eligible for co-option to the new educational body, Mary Bridges Adams was excluded as a potential troublemaker. From then on, she continued to pursue with vigour the cause of state education. In particular, she played a key role in extra-parliamentary campaigns in favour of the provision of school meals, medical inspection and treatment. The lack of women speakers and her experience of elected office meant that she frequently spoke at public meetings and her speeches were regularly reported in socialist newspapers, especially *Justice* (the organ of the Social Democratic Foundation).

After 1908 she was closely involved with the Marxist educators of the Plebs League and the labour colleges. Adult education was the battleground and Mary played a major role in the general promotion of a workers' education movement that was independent of the state and the class interests it represented. In her opinion, education led directly on to political action, and for this reason she argued for the inclusion of women in the new provision. To this end she met with partial success: securing limited funding for a separate women's college (named Bebel House after the German socialist) that quickly became financially untenable. Her involvement was covered by the educational journal, *Plebs*, in the form of letters, speeches and pamphlets.

When war broke out in August 1914 Mary's political energies took a new direction. A tireless opponent of the British war effort, she put her views forward in the *Cotton Factory Times* and the *Yorkshire Factory Times*. To leave it like that would be an understatement. To paraphrase Vickers, these papers literally were a 'goldmine of information'. In the war years she had something to say virtually every week (including Christmas and New Year), whether it be an article or a letter to the editor. At the same time, she was a less frequent contributor to *Clarion*, *Socialist* and Sylvia Pankhurst's *Woman's Dreadnought* (1914–17), superseded by *Worker's Dreadnought* (1917–24). For instance, she condemned the trial and imprisonment of John Maclean (perhaps the outstanding figure of the British revolutionary Left) and from 1915 to 1917 her home became the headquarters of the Committee of Delegates of Russian Socialist Groups in London. This brought her to the notice of the authorities and in 1917 she became an object of discussion in the House of Lords (see *Parliamentary Debates House of Lords*, 1917). In the opinion of the pro-war majority, she was a dangerous woman, and some of the documents that relate to her wartime activities remain covered by the Official Secrets Act. Unsurprisingly, Mary Bridges Adams alarmed many of those with whom she came into contact and this is reflected in her absence from the reminiscences and autobiographies of socialist politicians of this period. Similarly, visual material has been very hard to come by. There is the passport-sized photograph that accompanies the biographical feature in the *Illustrated London News*. Taken in middle age, she does not look directly at the camera, but the profile is attractive and she evidently had luxuriant hair. Ten years on, there is the *Daily Mirror* photo of two ladies in hats (Mary and the socialist Countess of Warwick) resplendent in an open carriage beside a report on the 1907 Trades Union Congress.

Closing the loop: the search for greater knowledge

In her day, Mrs Bridges Adams was nationally famous in the Labour movement but was quickly forgotten in the dominant narratives of the past. As with any other history, the stories of socialism share a preoccupation with the successful: successful organisations, leadership and ideologies. Part of the problem is that Bridges Adams left very little first-hand testimony. The personal papers are only fragments and her surviving letters are mostly short, tracked down in other collections of private papers such as those of the Labour leader George Lansbury (1859–1940). Yet she was a prolific writer of articles and letters and her national reputation as a speaker meant that her political activities were regularly reported. Some of those spoken words were also relayed in local newspapers. The most frustrating silence that has yet to be broken is with regard to the gaps in my knowledge of her early life. Birth and marriage certificates tell me where she lived at these moments in time but little else. Much more work remains to be done. Her public achievements are yet to be pieced together from related social and political history sources and the story is contingent upon new evidence being located.

Conclusion

Interesting and enlightening political research does not always rely upon the creation of new data. Many experienced and well-regarded political scientists conduct unique and illuminating research without having to engage with survey-creation or interview schedules. There is a wealth of historical and recently produced information which we can employ in political research – the two main problems involve location and existence. We cannot analyse data that do not exist, and this may inevitably influence the research questions we can realistically hope to answer.

In the last two chapters we have considered *types* of data format and *methods* of analysis which help us to integrate documentary material into our own research. We demonstrated in Chapter 7 that, although much of this material is qualitative in format, we can make use of both quantitative and qualitative techniques of analysis.

Content analysis is particularly useful for analysing the mass media, although such an approach tends to be descriptive rather than explanatory. We have briefly considered more qualitative approaches of analysis too (such as semiotics and discourse analysis) where the researcher moves away from a positivist research approach towards an explanation of meanings and influence.

In this chapter we have concentrated upon the strengths and limitations of using historical materials in political research. While we might take comfort from the fact that we cannot change the past, we can in fact offer alternative explanations and interpretations of who did what and why. What we have done is to explore some of the possibilities for such a research approach, while highlighting some of the pitfalls that political historians frequently encounter. Analysing existing data, rather than creating your own, is not a 'short-cut' to good research – it is time-consuming and inevitably frustrating when you discover that what you had expected to locate does not even exist. On the other hand, utilising historical data is rather like completing a jigsaw; and piecing together the previously neglected opinions, debates and actions can be extremely self-rewarding.

Further reading

J. Scott's text *A Matter of Record*, Cambridge: Polity Press, 1990, provides a good introduction to the use of documentary sources in general social research. For a quicker summary, see T. May, *Social Research: Issues, Methods and Process*, 2nd edn, Buckingham: Open University Press, 1997, ch. 8.

A. Seldon (ed.), *Contemporary History: Practice and Method*, Oxford: Basil Blackwell, 1988, provides an excellent collection of easy-to-read chapters on a range of sources. For a specifically political research-orientated account of archival research, see R. Vickers, 'Using Archives in Political Research', in P. Burnham (ed.), *Surviving the Research Process in Politics*, London: Pinter.

Deidre Beddoe has written a practical handbook *Discovering Women's History*, London: Pandora, 1983, which offers advice on how to locate and use a variety of sources to find out about the lives of ordinary women in Britain from 1800 to 1945.

Part III

DOING YOUR
OWN RESEARCH

Chapter 9

A guide to writing a politics dissertation

Introduction

So far, we have focused upon particular research methods – that is, the processes we engage in, and the specific techniques we make use of, in order to carry out political research. What I hope you have learnt is that the experience of carrying out research is influenced by a variety of issues and constraints. There is not necessarily a 'right' or 'wrong' way to address a research question, although there are 'more appropriate' methodological techniques and tools.

It is unusual for those engaging in undergraduate studies to be involved in operationalising large-scale research projects, although this is not to say you will not (or indeed, should not) engage in primary research (such as designing a questionnaire, carrying out a small-scale survey or interviewing political actors). However, such activities will be rather limited in scope compared to some of the 'real research' case studies which have been identified and explained in this text (such as the British Election Study or Heclo and Wildavsky's (1974) study of public expenditure).

The focus of this final section is two-fold. In the next chapter we shall identify some key sources of political data which you may find useful at different stages of your studies. In this chapter, however, we identify and examine some of the common concerns faced by dissertation students. This chapter does not seek to prescribe the *right way* of producing a high-quality dissertation. Indeed, different institutions and departments adopt many different rules and requirements (in relation to length, appropriate content and method of presentation). This said, the questions and concerns that dissertation students raise are very similar from year to year and from institution to institution. By at least taking into consideration the issues raised in this chapter, you should be able to avoid some common methodological mistakes.

What is a dissertation?

We may as well start at the beginning. There are probably as many definitions as Politics departments, although few would probably disagree with the following statement:

> a dissertation . . . is an extended piece of [political] analysis . . . [it] is the crystallisation of . . . [and] understanding of the methodological, theoretical and substantive debates . . . Finally, the dissertation is primarily a piece of independent research.
>
> (Adapted from *Dissertations in Sociology: Final Report*, University College Northampton, 1999)

The particular requirements and regulations for dissertations vary among different institutions, and it is vital that you familiarise yourself with these as early as possible (you may be allowed to look at previous submissions to gain a 'feel' for what a completed dissertation looks like). Yet the basic requirement of a dissertation is a lengthy piece of individual research which seeks to answer a particular, focused research question in a detailed, organised manner. This does not necessarily mean that each dissertation student has to find out something new, but it does mean that a dissertation should seek to take a *new perspective* on a research topic. This may entail the creation of new data (via a survey, by employing interviews, or by comparing existing data from different data sets). However, it is just as likely to involve a comparison and critical analysis of existing arguments and debates or of differing forms of texts.

It is worth bearing in mind that a dissertation should reflect *both specific* and *generic skills*. Generic skills apply equally to all dissertations: it is the ability to present a clear, structured argument which demonstrates an appreciation of the relevant information and appropriate writing skills. Specific skills should reflect the nature of the dissertation: being able to apply appropriate political theory(ies), operationalising appropriate methodological skills and developing knowledge in a particular research area.

Dissertation students often worry too much about originality, when in actual fact the most common weaknesses are that: the dissertation title is too broad (or indeed, not addressed); content tends to be descriptive rather than analytical; or the methods have not been sufficiently explained and justified (see Briefing box 9.1). It may be very easy, particularly if a large amount of existing literature is available, to summarise existing debates and arguments rather than focus strictly upon the research question. You might find that this is a particular concern when preparing your literature review: 'A very common problem found in literature reviews is the tendency to let them drift away from the rest of the dissertation and become separate scholarly essays' (Swetnam, 1995, p. 1).

We have shown in previous chapters that there is frequently more than one method of skinning a cat: research questions can lead to a range of answers, depending upon the methodological techniques employed. The same rule applies to dissertation titles (even though, due to practical constraints such as time and expense, it may appear quite obvious that only some avenues of research are feasible).

Briefing box 9.1 Common weaknesses identified in undergraduate dissertations

- The remit is too broad.
- The dissertation lacks sufficient analysis.
- There is poor justification of the methodology.
- There is unclear or contradictory use of terminology.

The rewards of independent research

Writing a dissertation can lead to very positive (but sometimes worrying) experiences. You are offered the opportunity to research something that really interests you (albeit with some well-founded advice from your supervisor). This may be something you have engaged with in a course already, or a topic in which you have developed an interest from elsewhere. Furthermore, you have the opportunity to get to know the subject area in quite some detail – by reading books, journal articles or indeed meeting relevant people – to a degree that is just not feasible in an average undergraduate course.

On the downside, writing a dissertation can be very lonely. Beyond meetings with your supervisor, you are unlikely to be able to participate in class discussions (and very few friends or family will exude nearly as much enthusiasm for the topic as you will!). There is always the worry that you have not encountered some vital source of information – a seminal text, a newly published journal article or some key documentary sources kept in a specialised library. Furthermore, what originally seemed like a fascinating topic can easily become boring and tedious. An analogy that springs to mind is working in a chocolate factory: it all looks tempting at first, but there comes a point when 'one more double-choc supreme' becomes rather nauseating. However, the chances are that you will only begin to reach this boredom threshold once you have conducted fairly detailed research.

As such, there are no hard and fast rules about what makes a good dissertation, but what we shall do here is examine some common issues raised by students, supervisors and examiners. Demonstrating some awareness of these issues (and addressing them in the production of a dissertation) will help you to justify how and why you have come to the conclusions that you reach.

Setting the research question

Perhaps the most important element of writing a successful dissertation is the title. Whatever methodological path you follow, ensure that the content of your dissertation does actually address the dissertation title/question. It is no use adopting a title such as *The Politics of Conservative Party Leadership Contests in the Twentieth Century* if you then find out that you only have evidence from the 1970s onwards, or that the topic is far too broad for the prescribed word limit. If you are not entirely confident of an exact title when you begin your research, start with a broad topic but be prepared to whittle this down, and discard interesting but tangentially relevant data where necessary.

It may be that you do not have an actual question to answer. This is not a problem as research can be either *deductive* or *inductive* in its formation of theory (see Chapter 1 for a broader discussion of these terms). If we take a deductive approach, we test, challenge or reinforce theory via conceptual analysis and reflection, 'drawing conclusions from first principles through a process of conceptual analysis and reflection' (Stoker, in Marsh and Stoker, 1995, p. 14). For example, if we decide to write a dissertation which asks: '*To what extent can the outcome of the 1997 General Election be explained by rational choice models of voting?*' we would be conducting deductive research – we are testing an existing theory that party preference is related to the voters' understanding of policies and the economic environment. In contrast, by adopting an inductive approach we develop a theory from empirical observation by identifying patterns and generalisations. Thus, a dissertation which asks: '*Why did the Conservative Party lose the 1997 General Election?*' would be taking an inductive approach. To answer this dissertation question we would look at the party's stance on a range of issues, as well as factors such as party cohesion and organisation. We may also find it useful to do the same with the party's competitors. As such, we are not suggesting that a particular explanation is right or wrong; instead we allow the data to decide. By examining the relevant evidence first, we are in a position to develop an explanation, then relate this to existing theory, or indeed develop new theory.

The chances are that you have chosen a dissertation topic because it is something you already know a little about, but about which you want to find out more. You might have a very particular, focused research question that you wish to examine or, as is often the case, you may have a more general theme that needs to be focused down. Some supervisors will help you to do this, although they may choose to advise alternative titles rather than prescribe a single one (I often talk to my students about what is feasible and what is more difficult to research but leave the ultimate choice to them as it is their project). Therefore, it is important to discuss the title with your supervisor and establish whether there is any flexibility in changing the title. It is useful to bear in mind that 'relatively few researchers end up studying precisely what they set out to study originally' (Blaxter *et al.*, 1996, p. 144).

Finally, be realistic about what research you can carry out. Remember, you have a word limit and probably have other assignments to complete at the same time. Producing small amounts of work at regular intervals quickly builds into a substantial body of work. The research that is feasible for an undergraduate dissertation is constrained by several factors, which are identified in Briefing box 9.2.

In relation to physical constraints, we have already mentioned that you will probably have to complete other study requirements whilst producing a dissertation. However, you may also encounter other hurdles, particularly if you are conducting an international study. While a visit to a UK library may be feasible, regular jaunts to the institutions of the European Union are unlikely to be as unproblematic. Cost may impact upon your research if you choose to carry out a survey. How much would it cost to photocopy 500 questionnaires? Do you need to distribute your survey via post? Can you afford to travel to a specialist library on more than one occasion?

It is not advisable to throw yourself into a research project when you have no experience of the necessary research techniques. If you recall the claims made in Chapter 6, interviewing was identified as a method which can involve many more complications than we might expect. Finally, do not 'assume' that sufficient literature exists for you to be able to write your dissertation. This is often a problem faced by

---

Briefing box 9.2 Potential constraints upon dissertation feasibility

- Physical (such as time or distance);
- cost;
- appropriate knowledge and experience of research techniques;
- appropriate supporting literature.

Source: Adapted from Swetnam (1995, p. 15)

---

students researching on-going political events (the peace process in Northern Ireland, for example). We stated in Chapter 8 that books and journal articles can take a considerable time to publish. This month's news story may seem interesting, but ask yourself whether there is a sufficient archive of relevant literature. Of course, a further limitation to literature may be a linguistic one. Discovering that the majority of texts produced on Latin American politics are not written in your main language can make the research process much more challenging than you first envisaged.

Where do I start with the research?

By establishing a title the work has already begun, because you have started to narrow down the field of data with which you can engage. A good starting point is a systematic bibliographic search, particularly as it helps us to learn from the successes, failures and ideas of others (Mannheim and Rich, 1995, p. 39).

Rather than collecting a single source of material at a time, and only looking for the next once we have read and digested each in detail, a much more appropriate method is to develop a wider appreciation of the research field by conducting a word or topic search. In the past, this had to be done by searching through bibliographies and collated indexes, but the task has been made much easier by the development of CD-ROMs and web sites which allow us to conduct quick searches of full-text newspaper articles and the plethora of bibliographical collections. However, a potential weakness of computer searches is that:

> First, the search is only as good as the key words we use. Second, the search is only as good as the data base it covers. Either or both of these factors can significantly limit the utility of a computer-generated bibliography.
>
> (Mannheim and Rich, 1995, p. 47)

If you refer back to our evaluation of content analysis in Chapter 7, we cited examples of how different words may be used to refer to the same or similar phenomenon (we considered research of the terms *sleaze* and *cronyism*). The same applies to a search for relevant texts. Think very carefully about the words and phrases you employ in a literature search. Phrases such as *elections*, *government* and *democratic* are probably too general and can generate hundreds, or indeed thousands, of 'hits'. Might very different words be used to describe the same phenomenon? Think of the case of public dissent in the late 1980s over the 'Poll Tax'. While this phrase is used in some texts and was the main term employed by the media, a bibliographic search should also demonstrate a recognition of its formal name – the Community Charge.

Of course, bibliographic searches are not restricted to events or phenomena. It is just as feasible to search by author (if you have found an article and want to see if the author has developed the debate further elsewhere). It is also possible to restrict searches to particular time spans. You may, for example, be interested in elections, but maybe only those that occurred in a certain decade. By searching for the term and a date, you can more effectively produce a list of relevant bibliographical sources.

Some texts, articles and even web sites will be of much greater value to your research than others. There are a variety of ways in which you may choose to take notes or 'remind' yourself of where you read something – hopefully you will have developed the system best suited to your own needs by the time you reach the dissertation stage. However, one aspect I do strongly recommend is that you take down *the full reference* for any book, article or web site as you are doing your reading. This is important for several reasons. First, constructing a bibliography is more time consuming than you think (this is someone who speaks from experience). Swetnam (1995, p. 17) claims that 5 per cent of research time is spent on producing the bibliography and (where applicable) appendices. There is nothing worse than spending a valuable afternoon sifting through library shelves and piles of photocopied material in order to find the date or place of publication. It is more efficient to take note of a reference as you proceed, and then find that you do not need that reference, than it is to construct a bibliography from scratch.

Second, you will not necessarily have access to all materials throughout the dissertation process; this is particularly the case if you have visited another library or archive, or if you have 'borrowed' material from your supervisor. Third, imagine you are relying heavily upon the work of one author (Professor J. Bloggs). You find that you have read a dozen books and articles by this author, and that at least three were published in the same year. Within your dissertation you have referred to particular points she makes and even include quotes to reinforce your argument. However, referencing as (Bloggs: 2000) is not sufficient, you will also need to use a letter reference system (such as 2000a, 2000b, 2000c). As long as you keep a full reference system as you prepare your dissertation, you will quickly become aware of the need for a systematic approach.

Issues to consider when the research is ongoing

So far, we have discussed the challenges that students confront when beginning their dissertation research. Deciding on a title and finding the relevant literature and/or data are just two of a wider range of issues we need to address when conducting our own research. In Briefing box 9.3, we outline further concerns that dissertation students might encounter.

Briefing box 9.3 Frequently encountered concerns in the dissertation process

- Level of supervision;
- data quality;
- access;
- integrating interview material;
- values and ethics.

The role of the supervisor

It is crucial that you establish at an early stage what level of support can be expected from your supervisor, and what other institutional provisions may be available which enable your own research. A frequent question asked is: 'How often should I see my supervisor?' Unfortunately, there is no hard and fast rule. Some supervisors may ask to see their tutees every week, others every month and others may advise you to show up only when you feel you need their guidance. Also, you may feel you need to see your supervisor more often as the completion date draws nearer. Many students find it useful to agree a progression timetable with their supervisor. It may, for example, motivate you to work on your dissertation if you have to deliver a new draft chapter to your supervisor at the end of each month (it is far too easy with a lengthy piece of work such as a dissertation to say 'I'll start work on it tomorrow').

You may find it useful to keep a 'log book' during the dissertation process (indeed, some institutions demand one). Writing down what you have discussed during a supervision meeting is invaluable (supervisors can be very frustrated by a student simply ignoring or forgetting their well-intentioned advice!). You may also use a log book to write down issues, questions and concerns as they arise between supervisory meetings which can then be addressed when you next meet (you will probably not remember all of them if you do not write them down). In terms of institutional support, find out if there are provisions and advice for dissertation students (is there the opportunity to develop IT skills, for example). What opportunities are there, if any, to access material which is not kept in the library? Do ask questions – there is nothing more frustrating than finding out about some invaluable provision when your dissertation deadline is looming!

The quality of research data

Within this text we have, at various stages, addressed the issues of 'right' or 'correct' methods. Indeed, the chances are that, while we can use a particular set of data to prove one theory, someone else can use a different set to prove the exact opposite. In Chapter 2 we addressed the issue of terminology and considered some of the expectations we have of research information. For example, we explained what it means to have data which is reliable and valid. How might these two concerns affect your dissertation work?

To recap, we can claim that our research findings are reliable if the data we employ give us the same result repeatedly. However, reliability can be undermined (or challenged) in a variety of ways. It could be that there are errors in producing the data (we do not add up survey results correctly, or we make errors when taking notes from documentary sources). Whilst our eventual claims may be correct, they are nevertheless undermined by incorrect evidence. A similar problem may derive from working with multi-definitional categories. We discussed in Chapter 4 the changing 'official' definition of unemployment. If we were to produce a dissertation examining *The Political Activity of the Unemployed* we would have to pay careful attention to how exactly we define the state of unemployment.

A common problem with dissertations is that multi-definitional terms are not clearly defined or that terms are used interchangeably. For example, there is a difference between the terms *political inactivity* and *political apathy*. It might be fair to assume that some people are politically inactive because they are apathetic towards politics; but there may be other reasons for political inactivity, such as resource availability and personal constraints. If you are using terms which are open to differing interpretations, make it clear that you are aware of this, and explain why you have chosen to use a particular definition (and make sure you consistently stick to this).

A third challenge to reliability is the issue of an 'understanding gap'. This is particularly applicable to dissertations which examine public opinion. Asking for opinions on the finer details of a particular government policy may be worthwhile if we are dealing with elites, but not the general public (for a further explanation, see the analysis of opinion polls in Chapter 3). In addition, data will quickly become unreliable if the respondent's interpretation of a question varies simply because he or she does not understand the issue being researched (Shively, 1998, p. 41). It is very important that you spend some time considering the most appropriate sources of data (both quantitative and qualitative) for investigating your research area – your supervisor should be able to help you here.

We chose, in Chapter 2, to accept the succinct definition offered by Mannheim and Rich (1995, p. 73), which states that validity is 'the extent to which our measures correspond to the concepts they are intended to reflect'. The external validity of research can be challenged, for example, when we make assumptions about a population which is derived from a non-representative sample (Kleinnjenhuis, in Pennings *et al.*, 1999, p. 86). It is unlikely that representative samples can be obtained in a dissertation study, so it is important that you do not try to make universally applicable claims.

Access

Anyone with any experience of research will have encountered problems of access. This may be a problem in terms of 'recorded' data – does your library contain all, or indeed any, texts on your research topic? In Chapter 4 we considered some of the practical hurdles that a researcher can face when attempting to access 'official' (that is, government created) data. You may find it useful, if visiting libraries outside of your own institution, to check opening hours and general restrictions upon access (Swetnam, 1995, p. 43).

Yet the restrictions we face in accessing published data are often not nearly as challenging as those we encounter when attempting to access 'private' information. For example, in Chapter 8 we considered the issue of private documents which may lie undiscovered for many years, or may possibly have been destroyed and are thus permanently inaccessible. In Chapter 6 we considered the hurdles faced by those wishing to interview political elites – such as identifying the 'gatekeepers'. Remember, you do not have any rights of admittance to the knowledge and thoughts of such people and any opportunity to utilise this research approach should be cherished and, more importantly, never exploited. I suggest you read carefully the case study in Chapter 6 if you are able to conduct interviews, and take note of the groundwork that is required. It is always a good idea to gain written confirmation that you have been granted access to interviews or personal papers (Swetnam, 1995, p. 15).

It may be easy (though mistaken) to assume that surveys provide a quicker and more favourable method of access. We have already suggested that this may not be appropriate in relation to the subject matter: in asking your friends and neighbours to comment upon the political situation in Tibet you may encounter some blank faces! (Remember, in Chapter 6 we referred to Lane's (1962) study in which he suggests that for one interviewee the terms 'politics' translates very strictly into the institution of government only.) Just because a two-page survey may be easier to complete than an hour-long interview, do not be fooled into believing that participants will be easy to recruit. Finding volunteers for your study can be crucial, but remember:

> The problem with volunteers is that they are not likely to be a random sample of the population. They tend to be better educated, of a higher social class, more intelligent, more social, less conforming and possess a higher need for approval than non-volunteers.
>
> (Burns, 2000, p. 18)

Two common problems encountered when using surveys are the effects of ambiguities and poor sampling. Swetnam (1995, p. 33) claims that: 'Students are often disappointed by very low response rates to their surveys but should realise that respondents may have little motivation to reply or may simply be irritated by the whole process if it is difficult to understand or too complex'; and furthermore: 'it is easier to obtain a one gramme sample from a tonne of limestone than to get an accurate sample of a hundred unemployed people' (ibid., p. 39).

You may decide to 'refresh' yourself on some of the practical issues surrounding survey research, which were discussed in some detail in Chapter 3. If you do choose to operationalise this methodological tool, you should strive to reduce the opportunity for non-completion and non-return. Think carefully about how you will retrieve completed questionnaires (are they to be filled in on the spot, left somewhere to be collected, or is a stamped addressed envelope provided?). Always be very clear about the purpose of the data collection: 'never distribute unheaded, unexplained questionnaires. As a minimum the heading should state the origin and purpose of the work' (Swetnam, 1995, p. 51).

Integrating interview material into your dissertation

Acquiring useful and enlightening data via qualitative interviews is challenging in itself, but it is important that you make appropriate use of it in your written analysis. If you recall that case study in Chapter 6, it was suggested that interview material may be organised in terms of 'a dialogue between you and your respondents'. Under each question, the range of respondents can be listed. Alternatively, responses can be organised by demographic variables (age group, level of political activity), although this is probably most useful for factual questions. Either approach provides 'a mesh of connections (difference/similarities) between your interviews'.

Yet merely inserting large chunks of verbatim interview material into your dissertation is not an advisable strategy. It can swallow up your word limit and leave the reader saying 'so what?'. It may be useful to code and summarise some of the general trends and more 'mundane' responses (for example, 'all interviewees decided to join party *x* after attending a rally with a friend' or '50 per cent indicated that they were unable to name their local MP'). In addition, direct quotations should be chosen for a purpose: to illustrate a difference or to aid in the justification of an explanation. The important point is to draw attention to all your findings as succinctly as possible (and relate them to the relevant theoretical underpinnings), but select quotations sparingly and use them to illustrate a point.

Ethics

At first sight you may be forgiven for thinking that ethics is not an issue which affects politics: sleaze and corruption are terms which have been applied to many political systems from time to time. However, it should not be assumed that ethics are alien to political research. Shively (1998) identifies several potential problems which can be encountered if we fail to address ethics within political research, and these are outlined in Briefing box 9.4.

You may feel that political research is unlikely to 'harm' individuals in the same way as experiments which involve psychological stress or physical deprivation. Dissertation students in psychology, for example, should be aware of and familiar with the requirements of the British Psychological Society which lays down fairly rigid recommendations in relation to research and ethics. We would no longer expect to see studies such as the one carried out in the 1930s, in which a United States-sponsored study by the Public Health Survey withheld treatment from 100 black syphilis sufferers in order to understand more about the course of the disease (Sapsford and Abbott, 1996, p. 318). Ethical considerations often underpin research involving children. In relation to political research, ethical expectations may be challenged when our employment of data breaks requirements of anonymity and confidentiality.

Briefing box 9.4 Ethical considerations when conducting political research

- Harm to subjects;
- embarrassment or psychological stress;
- imposition – particularly on public officials;
- confidentiality;
- fooling/misleading the subject – require consent.

Source: Shively (1998, p. 11)

Confidentiality is an issue we have discussed in earlier chapters, particularly in relation to qualitative studies involving interviews and personal documents (Seldon, 1988, p. 12). It is important that we make legitimate use of any new data, and this includes (as we recommended above) gaining permission for its publication. Remember, 'off the record' must mean precisely that (Blaxter *et al.*, 1997, p. 146). Similarly, it is no use identifying an interviewee as 'a female councillor' if it is easy to see that the particular council analysed has only one female councillor.

We must also be aware of demanding 'sensitive' information. Some people may be reluctant to divulge personal information – even when partaking in a large-scale survey in which their identity is never exposed. Commonly asked questions in social research which may demand potentially sensitive information are those which relate to age, ethnicity, marital status, sexuality, income, social class and level of education (ibid., p. 156). We may find that some people are rather reluctant to reveal their voting patterns (see the case study of opinion polling in Chapter 3), or may be reluctant to admit that they hold extremist or discriminatory views.

Finally, by being open and honest about the purpose of our research we may in fact encourage participation. It is important that participants 'trust' the research. In Chapter 4 we considered the pattern of a decline in public confidence in relation to the way in which government-collected data are used, and considered the suggestion that some people may have failed to register to vote because they assumed the data would be used in the collection of the Poll Tax (McLean and Smith, 1995). Misleading others to obtain any form of political data is not acceptable.

Conclusion

This chapter may appear to be a 'prophet of doom' in relation to the production of undergraduate dissertations, but this should not be the case. The secret of a good dissertation inevitably lies in the preparation as much as the written document, and I have merely sought to highlight some of the considerations which can influence your choice of research method(s). An inability to attain perfection should not discourage you from employing particular research approaches, but your supervisor will be much more supportive if you are at least able to recognise and deal with any problems you face, rather than if you simply sweep them under the carpet. I cannot overstate my earlier comment that dissertation research can be extremely rewarding – sufficient preparation will enable this to be the case.

Further reading

It is vital that you make full use of any dissertation guides and supporting materials that your institution provides. As I have mentioned, rules and requirements may vary among institutions. Make sure that you are familiar with you own institution's requirements at the beginning of the dissertation stage.

There are some general texts which may help you prepare your dissertation. For example, P. Creme and M. R. Lea, *Writing at University*, Buckingham: Open University Press, 1997, ch. 5 provides some useful hints on 'Reading as part of writing'. For a more holistic approach to dissertation writing, see D. Swetnam, *How To Write Your Dissertation*, Plymouth: How To Books, 1995.

For a broader discussion of access, see L. Blaxter, C. Hughes and M. Tight, *How to Research*, Buckingham: Open University Press, 1997, ch. 6.

For a broader discussion of the politics of social research, see the chapter by Sapsford and Abbott in R. Sapsford and V. Jupp (eds), *Data Collection and Analysis*, London: Sage, 1996.

Resources for political scientists

In this final chapter, we point to some useful sources of information for students and researchers in politics alike. The list is by no means exhaustive: there is a wealth of libraries, archives and web sites out there, and it would be impossible to include them all.

Those that are listed are chosen because they have proved to be invaluable to the authors of this text. Where possible, a short summary is provided to indicate what sort of information you can expect to find. Remember, these are nothing more than sources of information – we cannot guarantee that they will lead you to exactly the sort of data you wish to find, nor will they guarantee that your marks will be first class! They will, however, alert to you just a small section of the wealth of political data that are out there waiting to be discovered.

This chapter is divided into three sections. The first deals with 'printed guides'. There are volumes of almanacs and yearbooks produced, and data can quickly become obsolete. The chances are that your university library will have a selection of guides held in a 'Reference Only' section, and you may also find additional texts that are useful.

The second section lists a small selection of libraries and archives. These have been selected as a result of personal experience and are by no means intended to represent the 'best' or only resources of this type. The important factor you should bear in mind when attempting to use any library or archive is access. This may be something very simple such as opening times (no point in getting there when the doors are about to close), but you should also bear in mind that you may have to pre-book access, you may need some form of membership card or letter of introduction, and that not all sections of the library may be accessible to you. The general point to remember is that library and archival work can be extremely time-consuming. You may only become familiar with its workings after several visits. Generally speaking, you will be extremely fortunate if you can collect all the necessary data in a single visit.

The third section simply provides a list of 'useful' addresses and web sites. This covers academic sites, political parties, media resources, opinion pollsters, think tanks and other national and international organisations. Where possible, a full point of contact is provided (address, telephone and fax numbers, e-mail address and web site). In relation to political parties, the list is confined to those parties represented in the House of Commons, and a more detailed list can be found in *The British Elections and Parties Review*.

Accessing political data via the web is becoming increasingly easy and, in some cases, cheaper than relying upon printed texts. However, it is by no means a complete alternative, and you should treat some of the material available with caution (as we discussed in Chapter 7). You may find that some web sites are rather bland and lacking in substantive detail, others will not be in your first language, and web sites are not always updated at regular intervals (this may be problematic if you are looking for recent election data, for example). The web sites listed here are tried and tested, but their value for your own research will depend upon what exactly you want to know. All were accessed and live as of December 2000.

Printed texts

Public Records Office, *Record Repositories in Great Britain*, 11th edn, London: PRO, 1999. This handy guide provides a list of national, local, university and specialised repositories. Each entry is listed with full address and contact numbers (e-mail and web site references where appropriate), opening hours, conditions for entry and costs (if applicable).

J. Foster and J. Sheppard, *British Archives*, 3rd edn, Basingstoke: Macmillan, 1995.

This guide is similar in principle to the Public Records Office publication above, but much broader in terms of the institutions listed. It also includes a useful guide to 'Institutions which have placed archives elsewhere' and 'Institutions which have no archives'.

Dod's Parliamentary Companion 2000.

An invaluable guide to every detail you may (or may not) want to know about parliamentary politics in the UK. The current edition contains the Queen's Speech from 1999 and a complete list of Select Committee Reports. There are biographies of peers and MPs and election data from the 1997 General Election. The text includes information on government departments, the Scottish Parliament and Welsh and Northern Irish Assemblies, and provides a useful list of national and international organisations.

P. Cowley, D. Denver, A. Russell and L. Harrison (eds), *The British Elections and Parties Review*, Volume 10, London: Frank Cass, 2000.

Each volume of the *British Elections and Parties Review* contains a useful reference section. This includes a chronology of the year's events (1999 being the most recent), by-election results and the results of other relevant elections (local elections, Scottish and Welsh elections, European Parliamentary elections and party leadership elections), opinion poll data, a list of political party contacts and personnel, and national newspaper circulation.

R. Waller and B. Criddle, *The Almanac of British Politics*, 6th edn, London: Routledge, 1999.

Described as 'the definitive guide to the political map of the United Kingdom', this guide provides a profile of political constituencies and their representatives.

Libraries and archives

The British Library

The British Library has a main central library and several specialised libraries. The main library is located at:
96 Euston Road
London NW1 2DB
Tel: 020-7412-7332
e-mail: visitor-services@bl.uk

The British Library – Newspaper Library
Colindale Avenue
London NW9 5HE
Tel: 020-7412-7353
e-mail: newspaper@bl.uk
http://portico.bl.uk/collections/newpapers/

The British Library – National Sound Archive
Tel: 020-7421-7440
e-mail: nsa@bl.uk

BBC Written Archives Centre
Caversham Park
Reading
Berkshire PG4 8T2
Tel: 01734 472742
Fax: 01734 461145

British Library of Political and Economic Science
London School of Economics
10 Portugal Street
London WC2A 2HD
Tel: 020-7955-6733
http://www.blpes.lse.ac.uk

Fawcett Library (the national research library for women's history)
London Guildhall University
Calcutta House
Old Castle Street
London E1 7NT
Tel: 020-7320-1189
Fax: 020-7320-1188
e-mail: fawcett@lgu.ac.uk
http://www.lgu.ac.uk/fawcett/

Historical Manuscripts Commission (includes the UK National Register of
Archives)
Quality House
Quality Court
Chancery Lane
London WC2A AHP
Tel: 020-7242-1198
Fax: 020-7831-3550
e-mail: nra@hmc.gov.uk
http://www.hmc.gov.uk/main.htm

London Metropolitan Archives
40 Northampton Road
London EC1R OHB
http://www.cityoflondon.gov.uk/archives/lma

Modern Records Centre (includes trades union archives)
University of Warwick Library
Coventry CV4 7AL
http://www.warwick.ac.uk/services/library/mrc/mrc.shtml

Public Record Office
Ruskin Avenue
Kew
Richmond
Surrey TW9 4DU
Tel: 020-8392-5200
Fax: 020-8878-8905
e-mail: enquiry@pro.gov.uk
http://www.pro.gov.uk/

Working Class Movement Library
51 The Crescent
Salford M5 4WX
http://www.wcml.org.uk/

Addresses and web sites

Academic sites

Political Studies Association
PSA National Office
Department of Politics
University of Newcastle
Newcastle-Upon-Tyne NE1 7RU
Tel: 0191-222-8021

Fax: 0191-222-5069
e-mail: psa@ncl.ac.uk
http://www.psa.ac.uk/
This is an excellent site which claims to have links to 'over 3000 political information sources on the internet'. There are links by theme (see below) and also a search engine. The following categories have easy links:

- constitutions
- gender and politics
- politics departments
- elections

- data archives
- libraries and archives
- politics resources

- journals
- media
- world

British International Studies Association (BISA)
http://www.bisa.ac.uk/

Similar in principle to the PSA, but focuses upon international relations, media resources, opinion pollsters, think tanks and international organisations.

Political parties

Conservative and Unionist Central Office
32 Smith Square
Westminster
London SW1P 3HH
Tel: 020-7222-9000
Fax: 020-7222-1135
http://www.conservative-party.org.uk

The Labour Party
Millbank Tower
Millbank
London SW1P 4GT
Tel: 08705-900-200
Fax: 020-7802-1555
e-mail: labour-party@geo2.poptel.org.uk
http://www.labour.org.uk

The Liberal Democrats
Party Headquarters
4 Cowley Street
London SW1P 3NB
Tel: 020-7222-7999
Fax: 020-7799-2170
e-mail: libdems@cix.co.uk
http://www/libdems.org.uk

Scottish National Party
107 McDonald Road
Edinburgh EH7 4NW
Tel: 0131-525-8900
Fax: 0131-525-8901
e-mail: snp.hq@snp.org
http://www.snp.org

Plaid Cymru
18 Park Grove
Cardiff CF10 3BN
Tel: 02920 646000
Fax: 02920 646001
e-mail: post@plaidcymru.org
http://www.plaid-cymru.org

Democratic Unionist Party
91 Dundela Avenue
Belfast BT4 3BU
Tel: 028-9047-1155
Fax: 028-9047-1797
e-mail: info@dup.org.uk
http://www.dup.org.uk

Sinn Féin
Belfast Headquarters:
51–55 Falls Road
Belfast BT13
Tel: 01232-624-421
Fax: 01232-622-112

Dublin Office:
44 Cearnóg Pharnell (Parnell Square)
Dublin 1
Republic of Ireland
Tel: (00) 3531-872-6100/872-6939
Fax: (00) 3531-873-3074
e-mail: sinnfein@iol.ie
http://www.sinnfein.ie/index.html

Social Democratic and Labour Party
121 Ormeau Road
Belfast BT7 1SH
Tel: 028-9024-7700
Fax: 028-9023-6699
e-mail: sdlp@indigo.ie
http://www.sdlp.ie

UK Unionist Party
10 Hamilton Road
Bangor BT20 4LE
Tel: 01247 479538
Fax: 01247 465037
e-mail: info@ukup.org
http://www.ukup.org

Ulster Unionist Party
3 Glengall Street
Belfast BT12 5AE
Tel: 028-9032-4601
Fax: 028-9024-6738
e-mail: uup@uup.org
http://www.uup.org

The mass media

BBC   http://www.bbc.co.uk/
ITN   http://www.itn.co.uk/
Guardian   http://www.guardianunlimited.co.uk/
Independent   http://www.independent.co.uk/
The Scotsman   http://www.scotsman.com/
Telegraph   http://www.telegraph.co.uk/
The Times   http://www.thetimes.co.uk/

Opinion polls

The Gallup Organisation Ltd
Drapers Court
Kingston Hall Road
Kingston-upon-Thames
Surrey KT1 2BG
Tel: 020-8939-7000
Fax: 020-8939-7039
http://www/gallup.com

MORI
95 Southwark Street
London SE1 0HX
Tel: 020-7928-5955
Fax: 020-7955-0067
e-mail: mori@mori.com
http://www.mori.com

Think tanks

The Adam Smith Institute
PO Box 316
London SW1P 3DJ
Tel: 020-7222-4995
Fax: 020-7222-7544
e-mail: info@adamsmith.org.uk
http://www.adamsmith.org.uk

Demos
The Mezzanine
Elizabeth House
9 York Road
London SE1 7NQ
Tel: 020-7401-5330
Fax: 020-7401-5331
e-mail: mail@demos.co.uk
http://www.demos.co.uk

Fabian Society
11 Dartmouth Street
London SW1H 9BH
Tel: 020-7227-4900
Fax: 020-7976-7153
e-mail: info@fabian-society.org.uk
http://www.fabian-society.org.uk

The Institute for Public Policy Research
30–32 Southampton Street
London WC2E 7RA
Tel: 020-7470-6100
Fax: 020-7470-6111
e-mail: info@ippr.org.uk
http://www.ippr.org.uk

National organisations

Acts of UK Parliament   http://www.hmso.gov.uk/acts.htm
This site provides a link to the full text of Public General Acts (since 1988), Local Acts
(since 1991) and Bills currently before the UK Parliament.

Centre for Applied Social Surveys (CASS)   http://www.natcen.ac.uk/cass/
CASS 'is an ESRC Resource Centre run jointly by The National Centre for Social
Research and the University of Southampton, with the University of Surrey'. There
are a wide range of links to domestic and international sites dealing with survey

research, and you can access some of the national surveys which have been mentioned in this text (such as the *Labour Force Survey* and the *British Elections Surveys*).

ESRC Qualitative Data Archival Resource Centre
Department of Sociology
University of Essex
Colchester CO4 3SQ
Tel: 01206 873058
Fax: 01206 873410
e-mail: quali@essex.ac.uk
http://www.essex.ac.uk/qualidata/

For those favouring a qualitative approach to research, this web site has been constructed 'to facilitate and document the archiving of qualitative data arising from research'.

Government http://www.open.gov.uk/
The homepage claims to be 'a first entry point to UK public sector information on the internet', and is organised according to public sector bodies.

The Local Government Association
Local Government House
Smith Square
London SW1P 3HZ
Tel: 020-7664-3000
Fax: 020-7664-3030
e-mail: info@lga.gov.uk
http://www.lga.gov.uk

National statistics http://www.statistics.gov.uk

United Kingdom Parliament http://www.parliament.uk/
This web site claims to provide information 'about the United Kingdom Parliament, the House of Commons and the House of Lords'. There are links to 'business, publications, and information about members and committees'.

International organisations

EURODATA http://www.mzes.uni-mannheim.de/eurodata/frm_eurodata.html
The EURODATA Research Archive is based in Mannheim and contains socio-economic and political data at the aggregate level. Its basic function is to support comparative European research.

Europa http://europa.eu.int/
A web page for those interested in the European Union, it claims to 'provide up-to-date coverage of European Union affairs and essential information on European

integration'. There are links to institutions, official documents and publications, and relevant statistics.

International Labour Organisation
http://www.ilo.org/public/english/index. htm

Organisation for Economic Co-operation and Development (OECD)
http://www.oecd.org/

United Nations   http://www.un.org/

Glossary

aggregate data   Quantitative data collected at the population level in order to identify changes and trends, such as government statistics. We cannot extrapolate individual patterns from the aggregate level.

causality   Within quantitative research we often discuss our analysis in terms of variables which may or may not influence political outcomes. The ability of a characteristic (or variable) to affect attitudes or behaviour is referred to as causality.

content analysis   Technique used to study patterns of information in printed and broadcast matter. Often used in studies of representations in the media.

correlation   Measures the extent to which the changes which occur in two variables or attributes are associated with one another. A correlation exists if a change in the independent variable leads to a similar change in a dependent variable.

cultural relativism   The rules of political and social behaviour which influence the manner in which that system is constructed and operates.

deductive approach   The development of claims or hypotheses from existing theory. The research develops as a 'test' of what we might 'expect' to find.

diachronic   A diachronic definition is one that changes in meaning over time as a result of historical, cultural and social change (poverty, for example).

ecological fallacy   A problem faced if attempting to draw false conclusions about individuals from aggregate data.

elite survey   A methodological approach to obtaining information from a group of political actors whose occupation or knowledge deems them to be important.

ethnocentrism   The problem of assessing different political cultures and societies by one's own values and expectations.

ethnography   A research principle stating that social reality can only be understood by directly experiencing that reality.

focus group A methodological tool which can be employed at various stages in the research process. A focus group consists of 8–10 participants who discuss a topic in depth. The detail of the discussion and the interaction between subjects are important aspects of the analysis.

gatekeepers Those who control access to research data (for example, to interviewees, documents and archives).

inductive approach An alternative to the deductive approach. The building of theory as a result of empirical findings.

inference An inference is made when a small sample is used to make judgements about the larger population.

mass survey A survey which targets the general population, unlike elite surveys.

pilot study A 'dummy run' of intended research carried out in order to identify potential problems with the proposed research design.

population The total group sharing the common characteristics which it is wished to study, for example, party members, non-voters. The population forms the sampling frame from which samples can be drawn.

primary analysis Analysis of data which is 'first hand'. Our analysis is not affected by the earlier established interpretations of others.

questionnaire A list of questions which forms the methodological tool for conducting a survey.

reactivity Alteration in the behaviour of research participants as a reaction to the knowledge that they are being studied.

reliability Research findings are reliable if they can be replicated.

response set A problem encountered in survey research; the tendency for participants to repeat their responses to a list of questions (such as attitude scales), rather than providing 'genuine' responses.

sampling The process by which we select cases to study if we are unable to analyse the entire research population. There are two main approaches: probabilistic and non-probabilistic sampling.

secondary analysis The analysis of data which have already been interpreted by another.

significance When conducting quantitative research statistical tests and 'levels of significance' may be used to test the confidence or certainty of the research findings, although there is never absolutely certainty that the findings are correct.

survey A methodological approach to collecting factual and attitude data from a large sample. The data gathered via questionnaires form the survey.

triangulation A process by which two or more kinds of data from different sources are used to see if the information is corroborated.

understanding gap The responses those being researched give to surveys/interviews may not be 'genuine'. For example, a respondent may give a different response to the same question at different times because he/she has little understanding/knowledge of the research topic, rather than because there has been a real change in attitude/opinion.

validity A measure is valid if it measures what it claims to measure, for example, a relationship really does exist between the concept and the measure. Research can be reliable (repeatable) but not necessarily valid.

variable In political research we are interested in the relationship between *variables*. For example, in a survey we might find out that certain people vote for party *x*, and we wish to find out the reasons why this group is prone to behave in this way. As such, voting behaviour is a *dependent variable* that may be influenced by a range of *independent variables*, such as age, gender and class.

Bibliography

Bale, T. (1996) 'Interview Material in Political Science', *Politics*, 16 (1): 63–67.

Barnes, J. (1988) 'Books and Journals', in A. Seldon, *Contemporary History: Practice and Method*, Oxford: Blackwell.

Bartle, J. (1999) 'Improving the Measurement of Party Identification in Britain', in J. Fisher, P. Cowley, D. Denver and A. Russell (eds), *The British Elections and Parties Review*, Volume 9, London: Frank Cass.

Beddoe, D. (1983) *Discovering Women's History: A Practical Manual*, London: Pandora.

Bernstein, R.A. and Dyer, J.A. (1992) *An Introduction to Political Science Methods*, 3rd edn, Englewood Cliffs, NJ: Prentice-Hall.

Black, T.R. (1993) *Evaluating Social Science Research*, London: Sage.

Blair, A. (1999) 'Question Time: Questionnaires and Maastricht', *Politics*, 19 (2): 117–124.

Blakemore, M. (1999) 'Working with Government to Disseminate Official Statistics', in D. Dorling and S. Simpson (eds), *Statistics in Society: The Arithmetic of Politics*, London: Arnold.

Blaxter, L., Hughes, C. and Tight, M. (1996) *How to Research*, Buckingham: Open University Press.

Blondel, J. (1976) *Thinking Politically*, Harmondsworth: Penguin.

Borg, W.R. (1963) *Educational Research: An Introduction*, London: Longman.

Brand, J., Mitchell, J. and Surridge, P. (1994) 'Social Constituency and Ideological Profile: Scottish Nationalism in the 1990s', *Political Studies*, 42 (4): 616–629.

Broughton, D. (1995) *Public Opinion Polling and Politics in Britain*, Hemel Hempstead: Harvester Wheatsheaf.

Broughton, D. (1998) 'Chronology of Events 1997', in D. Denver, J. Fisher, P. Cowley and C. Pattie (eds), *The British Elections and Parties Review*, Volume 8: *The 1997 General Election*, London: Frank Cass.

Budge, I. (1999) 'Party Policy and Ideology: Reversing the 1950s?', in G. Evans and P. Norris (eds), *Critical Elections: British Parties and Voters in Long-term Perspective*, London: Sage.

Bulmer, M. (ed.) (1982) *Social Research Ethics*, London: Macmillan.

Burnham, P. (ed.) (1997) *Surviving the Research Process in Politics*, London: Pinter.

Burns, R.B. (2000) *Introduction to Research Methods*, 4th edn, London: Sage.

Butler, D. and Butler, G. (1994) *British Political Facts 1900–1994*, London: Macmillan.

Butler, D. and Kavanagh, D. (1992) *The British General Election of 1992*, Basingstoke: Macmillan.

Butler, D. and Kavanagh, D. (1997) *The British General Election of 1997*, Basingstoke: Macmillan.

Butler, D. and Stokes, D. (1971) *Political Change in Britain: Forces Shaping Electoral Choice*, Harmondsworth: Penguin.

Calder, J. (1996) 'Statistical Techniques', in R. Sapsford and V. Jupp (eds), *Data Collection and Analysis*, London: Sage.

Childs, D. (1992) *Britain since 1945: A Political History*, 3rd edn, London: Routledge.

Clark, A. (1994) *Diaries*, London: Phoenix.

Clarke, H., Stewart, M.C. and Whiteley, P. (1999) 'New Labour's New Partisans: The Dynamics of Party Identification in Britain since 1992', in J. Fisher, P. Cowley, D. Denver and A. Russell (eds), *The British Elections and Parties Review*, Volume 9, London: Frank Cass.

Cole, J. (1995) *As It Seemed to Me*, London: Weidenfeld & Nicolson.

Converse, P.E. (1964) 'The Nature of Belief Systems in Mass Publics', in D. Apter (ed.), *Ideology and Discontent*, New York: Free Press.

Corston, R. and Colman, A. (2000) *A Crash Course in SPSS for Windows*, Oxford: Blackwell.

Cox, N. (1988) 'Public Records', in A. Seldon (ed.), *Contemporary History: Practice and Method*, Oxford: Blackwell.

Craig, F.W.S. (1989) *British Electoral Facts, 1832–1987*, Aldershot, Hants.: Dartmouth.

Creme, P. and Lea, M.R. (1997) *Writing at University*, Buckingham: Open University Press.

Crewe, I. (1997) 'The Opinion Polls: Confidence Restored?', in P. Norris and N. T. Gavin (eds), *Britain Votes 1997*, Oxford: Oxford University Press.

Curtice, J. (1997) 'So How Well Did They Do? The Polls in the 1997 Election', *Journal of the Market Research Society*, 39 (3): 449–461.

Dahl, R.A. (1961) 'The Behavioral Approach in Political Science: Epitaph for a Monument to a Successful Protest', *American Political Science Review*, 55: 763–772.

Dale, A. (1999) 'Confidentiality of Official Statistics: an Excuse for Secrecy', in D. Dorling and S. Simpson (eds), *Statistics in Society: The Arithmetic of Politics*, London: Arnold.

Dale, A., Arber, S. and Procter, M. (1988) *Doing Secondary Analysis*, London: Unwin.

Dargie, C. (1998) 'Observation in Political Research', *Politics*, 18 (1): 65–71.

Day, S. (1997) 'Breaking Free Through the Use of Unusual Sources', in P. Burnham (ed.), *Surviving the Research Process in Politics*, London: Pinter.

Denman, J. (1994) 'How Exactly Is Unemployment Measured?', *Statistical News*, 106 (Autumn).

Denver, D., Fisher, J., Cowley, P. and Pattie, C. (eds) (1998) *British Elections and Parties Review*, volume 8: *The 1997 Gneral Election*, London: Frank Cass.

Devine, F. (1992) 'Working-class Evaluations of the Labour Party', in I. Crewe, P. Norris, D. Denver and D. Broughton (eds), *British Elections and Parties Yearbook 1991*, Hemel Hempstead: Harvester Wheatsheaf.

Devine, F. (1992a) *Affluent Workers Revisited: Privatism and the Working Class*, Edinburgh: Edinburgh University Press.

Devine, F. (1994) 'Learning More About Mass Political Behaviour: Beyond Dunleavy', in D. Broughton, D. Farrell, D. Denver and C. Rallings (eds), *British Elections and Parties Yearbook 1994*, London: Frank Cass.

Devine, F. (1995) 'Qualitative Analysis', in D. Marsh and G. Stoker (eds), *Theory and Methods in Political Science*, London: Macmillan.

Diamond, I. (1999) 'The Census', in D. Dorling and S. Simpson (eds), *Statistics in Society: The Arithmetic of Politics*, London: Arnold.

Doig, A., McIvor, S. and Moran, J. (1999) 'A Word Desperately Seeking Scandal? New Labour and Tony's Cronies', *Parliamentary Affairs*, 52 (4): 676–687.

Dorling, D. and Simpson, S. (eds) (1999) *Statistics in Society: The Arithmetic of Politics*, London: Arnold.

Dowse, R. and Hughes, J. (1986) *Political Sociology*, Chichester: John Wiley.

Dunleavy, P. (1990) 'Mass Political Behaviour: Is There More to Learn?', *Political Studies*, 38 (2): 453–469.

Eldridge, J. (ed.) (1995) *Glasgow Media Group Reader*, Volume 1: *News Content, Language and Visuals*, London: Routledge.

Evans, G. and Norris, P. (eds) (1999), *Critical Elections: British Parties and Voters in Long-term Perspective*, London: Sage.

Fielding, J. and Gilbert, N. (2000) *Understanding Social Statistics*, London: Sage.

Fielding, N. (1982) 'Observational Research on the National Front', in M. Bulmer (ed.), *Social Research Ethics*, London: Macmillan.

Finch, J. (1993) 'It's Great to Have Someone to Talk to: Ethics and Politics of Interviewing Women's Experience', in M. Hammersley (ed.), *Social Research: Philosophy, Politics and Practice*, London: Sage.

Finer, S.E. (1987) *Comparative Government: An Introduction to the Study of Politics*, Harmondsworth, Middx: Penguin.

Finnegan, R. (1996) 'Using Documents', in R. Sapsford and V. Jupp (eds), *Data Collection and Analysis*, London: Sage.

Fiske, J. and Hartley, J. (1996) *Reading Television*, London: Routledge.

Flickinger, R.S. (1995) 'British Political Parties and Public Attitudes Towards the European Community: Leading, Following or Getting Out of the Way?', in D. Broughton, D. Farrell, D. Denver and C. Rallings (eds), *British Elections and Parties Yearbook 1994*, London: Frank Cass.

Foster, P. (1996) 'Observational Research', in R. Sapsford and V. Jupp (eds), *Data Collection and Analysis*, London: Sage.

Gaber, I. (1998) 'Debate on Section 93 of the Representation of the People Act. The Case Against: Scrap It', in I. Crewe, B. Gosschalk and J. Bartle (eds), *Political Communications: Why Labour Won the General Election of 1997*, London: Frank Cass.

Gamble, A. (1994) 'Political Memoirs', *Politics*, 14 (1): 35–41.

Geddes, A. and Tonge, J. (eds) (1997) *Labour's Landslide*, Manchester: Manchester University Press.

Gibson, R. and Ward, S. (2000) 'An Outsider's Medium? The European Elections and UK Party Competition on the Internet', in P. Cowley, D. Denver, A. Russell and L. Harrison (eds), *British Elections and Parties Review*, Volume 10, London: Frank Cass.

Goddard, E. (1999) 'Public Confidence in Official Statistics', *Statistical News*, 124 (Summer).

Goddard, P., Scammell, M. and Semetko, H. (1998) 'Too Much of a Good Thing? Television in the 1997 Election Campaign', in I. Crewe, B. Gosschalk and J. Bartle (eds), *Political Communications: Why Labour Won the General Election of 1997*, London: Frank Cass.

Gould, P. (1998) *The Unfinished Revolution*, London: Little, Brown.

Government Statisticians' Collective (1993) 'How Official Statistics are Produced: Views from the Inside', in M. Hammersley (ed.), *Social Research: Philosophy, Politics and Practice*, London: Sage.

Guy, W. (1996) 'Health for All?', in R. Levitas and W. Guy (eds), *Interpreting Official Statistics*, London: Routledge.

Hakim, C. (1993) 'Research Analysis of Administrative Records', in M. Hammersley (ed.), *Social Research: Philosophy, Politics and Practice*, London: Sage.

Halfpenny, P. (1984) *Principles of Method*, York: Longman.

Hammersley, M. (ed.) (1993) *Social Research: Philosophy, Politics and Practice*, London: Sage.

Harrison, L. and Deicke, W. (2000) 'Capturing the First Time Voters: an Initial Study of Political Attitudes among Teenagers', *Youth and Policy*, 67, 26–40.

Heath, A. and Pierce, R. (1992) 'It Was Party Identification All Along: Question Order Effects on Reports of Party Identification in Britain', *Electoral Studies*, 11 (2): 93–105.

Heath, A., Jowell, R. and Curtice, J. (1994) *Labour's Last Chance? The 1992 Election and Beyond*, Aldershot: Dartmouth.

Heclo, H. and Wildavsky, A. (1974) *The Private Government of Public Money*, London: Macmillan.

Hennessy, P. (1988) 'The Press and Broadcasting', in A. Seldon (ed.), *Contemporary History: Practice and Method*, Oxford: Blackwell.

Hollis, P. (1997) *Jennie Lee: A Life*, Oxford: Oxford University Press.

Howarth, D. (1998) 'Discourse Theory and Political Analysis', in E. Scarbrough and E. Tanenbaum (eds), *Research Strategies in the Social Sciences*, Oxford: Oxford University Press.

Howe, G. (1995) *Conflict of Loyalty*, Basingstoke: Pan.

Jowell, R., Curtice, J., Park, A. and Thomson, K. (eds) (1999) British Social Attitudes 16th Report: *Who Shares New Labour's Values?*, Aldershot: Ashgate.

Jupp, V. (1996) 'Documents and Critical Research', in R. Sapsford and V. Jupp (eds), *Data Collection and Analysis*, London: Sage.

Jupp, V. and Norris, C. (1993) 'Traditions in Documentary Analysis', in M. Hammersley (ed.), *Social Research: Philosophy, Politics and Practice*, London: Sage.

King, A., Denver, D., McLean, I., Norris, P., Sanders, D. and Seyd, P. (1998) *New Labour Triumphs: Britain at the Polls*, London: Chatham House.

Lane, R. (1962) *Political Ideology: Why the American Common Man Believes What He Does*, New York: Free Press of Glencoe.

Lee, P. (1999) 'Where Are the Deprived? Measuring Deprivation in Cities and Region', in D. Dorling and S. Simpson (eds), *Statistics in Society: The Arithmetic of Politics*, London: Arnold.

Levitas, R. (1996a) 'The Legacy of Rayner', in R. Levitas and W. Guy (eds), *Interpreting Official Statistics*, London: Routledge.

Levitas, R. (1996b) 'Fiddling While Rome Burns? The "Measurement" of Unemployment', in R. Levitas and W. Guy (eds), *Interpreting Official Statistics*, London: Routledge.

Levitas, R. and Guy, W. (eds) (1996) *Interpreting Official Statistics*, London: Routledge.

Levy, M. (1996) 'Modernization and the Clause IV Reform: the Attitudes of Labour Backbench MPs', in D.M. Farrell, D. Broughton, D. Denver and J. Fisher (eds), *The British Elections and Parties Yearbook 1996*, London: Frank Cass.

Lippman, W. (1922) *Public Opinion*, New York: Harcourt Brace.

Macfarlane, A. and Head, J. (1999) 'What Do Official Health Statistics Measure?', in D. Dorling and S. Simpson (eds), *Statistics in Society: The Arithmetic of Politics*, London: Arnold.

Mackie, T. and Marsh, D. (1995) 'The Comparative Method', in D. Marsh and G. Stoker (eds), *Theory and Methods in Political Science*, London: Macmillan.

Mannheim, J.B. and Rich, R.C. (1995) *Empirical Political Analysis: Research Methods in Political Science*, 4th edn, New York: Longman.

Market Research Society Working Party (1994) *The Opinion Polls and the 1992 General Election*, London: Market Research Society.

Marsh, D and Stoker, G. (eds) (1995) *Theory and Methods in Political Science*, London: Macmillan.

May, T. (1993) *Social Research: Issues, Methods and Process*, Buckingham: Open University Press.

May, T. (1997) *Social Research: Issues, Methods and Process*, 2nd edn, Buckingham: Open University Press.

McLean, I. and Bustani, C. (1999) 'Irish Potatoes and British Politics: Interests, Ideology, Heresthetic and the Repeal of the Corn Laws', *Political Studies*, 47 (5): 817–836.

McLean, I. and Smith, J. (1995) 'The Poll Tax, the Electoral Register, and the 1991 Census: an Update', in D. Broughton, D. Farrell, D. Denver and C. Rallings (eds), *British Elections and Parties Yearbook 1994*, London: Frank Cass.

McRobbie, A. (2000) *Feminism and Youth Culture*, 2nd edn, Basingstoke: Macmillan.

Miles, R. (1989) *The Women's History of the World*, London: Paladin.

Miller, W. (1995) 'Quantitative Methods', in D. Marsh and G. Stoker (eds), *Theory and Methods in Political Science*, London: Macmillan.

Moon, N. (1999) *Opinion Polls: History, Theory and Practice*, Manchester: Manchester University Press.

Negrine, R. (1989) *Politics and the Mass Media in Britain*, London: Routledge.

Newton, K. (1992) 'Do People Read Everything They Believe in the Papers? Newspapers and Voters in the 1983 and 1987 Elections', in I. Crewe, P. Norris, D. Denver and D. Broughton (eds), *British Elections and Parties Yearbook 1991*, Hemel Hempstead: Harvester Wheatsheaf.

Nichols, T. (1996) 'Social Class: Official, Sociological and Marxist', in R. Levitas and W. Guy (eds), *Interpreting Official Statistics*, London: Routledge.

Noelle-Neuman, E. (1984) *The Spiral of Silence*, Chicago: University of Chicago Press.

Norris, P. (ed.) (1997a) *Passages to Power*, Cambridge: Cambridge University Press.

Norris, P. (1997b) *Electoral Change since 1945*, Oxford: Blackwell.

Norris, P. (1998) 'The Battle for the Campaign Agenda', in A. King *et al.*, *New Labour Triumphs: Britain at the Polls*, London: Chatham House.

Norris, P. and Gavin, N. (1997) *Britain Votes 1997*, Oxford: Oxford University Press.

Norris, P. and Lovenduski, J. (1995) *Political Recruitment: Gender, Race and Class in the British Parliament*, Cambridge: Cambridge University Press.

Norris, P., Curtice, J., Sanders, D., Scammell, M. and Semetko, H.A. (1999) *On Message: Communicating the Campaign*, London: Sage.

Nossiter, T.J., Scammell, M. and Semetko, H. (1995) 'Old Values versus News Values: the British 1992 General Election Campaign on Television', in I. Crewe and B. Gosschalk (eds), *Political Communications: The General Election Campaign of 1992*, Cambridge: Cambridge University Press.

Owen, C. (1999) 'Government Household Surveys', in D. Dorling and S. Simpson (eds), *Statistics in Society: The Arithmetic of Politics*, London: Arnold.

Page, E. (1990) 'British Political Science and Comparative Politics', *Political Studies*, 38 (2): 438–452.

Pennings, P., Keman, H. and Kleinnijenhuis, J. (1999) *Doing Research in Political Science: An Introduction to Comparative Methods and Statistics*, London: Sage.

Perrons, D. (1999) 'Missing Subjects? Searching for Gender in Official Statistics', in D. Dorling and S. Simpson (eds), *Statistics in Society: The Arithmetic of Politics*, London: Arnold.

Philo, G. (1990) *Seeing and Believing: The Influence of Television*, London: Routledge.

Povey, D. (1995) 'Truths, Home Truths and Crime Statistics', *Statistical News*, 107 (Spring).

Punch, M. (1993) 'Observation and the Police: the Research Experience', in M. Hammersley (ed.), *Social Research: Philosophy, Politics and Practice*, London: Sage.

Raspin, A. (1988) 'Private Papers', in A. Seldon (ed.), *Contemporary History: Practice and Method*, Oxford: Blackwell.

Reid, S. (1987) *Working with Statistics*, Oxford: Polity Press.

Rentoul, J. (1997) *Tony Blair*, London: Warner Books.

Richards, D. (1996) 'Elite Interviewing: Approaches and Pitfalls', *Politics*, 16 (3): 199–204.

Rose, D. and Sullivan, O. (1993) *Introducing Data Analysis for Social Scientists*, Buckingham: Open University Press.

Rose, R. (1991) 'Comparing Forms of Comparative Analysis', *Political Studies*, 39 (3): 446–462.

Samuels, A. (1993) *The Political Psyche*, London: Routledge.

Sanders, D. (1999) 'The Impact of Left–Right Ideology', in G. Evans and P. Norris (eds), *Critical Elections: British Parties and Voters in Long-term Perspective*, London: Sage.

Sapsford, R. and Abbott, P. (1996) 'Ethics, Politics and Research', in R. Sapsford and V. Jupp (eds), *Data Collection and Analysis*, London: Sage.

Sapsford, R. and Jupp, V. (eds) (1996) *Data Collection and Analysis*, London: Sage.

Scammell, M. and Harrop, M. (1997) 'The Press', in D. Butler and D. Kavanagh (eds), *The British General Election of 1997*, Basingstoke: Macmillan.

Scarbrough, E. and Tanenbaum, E. (1998) *Research Strategies in the Social Sciences*, Oxford: Oxford University Press.

Schofield, J.W. (1993) 'Increasing the Generalizability of Qualitative Research Experience', in M. Hammersley (ed.), *Social Research: Philosophy, Politics and Practice*, London: Sage.

Schofield, W. (1996) 'Survey Sampling', in R. Sapsford and V. Jupp (eds), *Data Collection and Analysis*, London: Sage.

Scott, J. (1990) *A Matter of Record*, Cambridge: Polity Press.

Seale, C. (ed.) (1998) *Researching Society and Culture*, London: Sage.

Seldon, A. (ed.) (1988) *Contemporary History: Practice and Method*, Oxford: Blackwell.

Semetko, H., Scammell, M. and Nossiter, T.J. (1994) 'The Media's Coverage of the Campaign', in A. Heath, R. Jowell, and J. Curtice (eds), *Labour's Last Chance? The 1992 Election and Beyond*, Aldershot: Dartmouth.

Seyd, P. (1999) 'New Parties/ New Politics: a Case Study of the British Labour Party?', *Party Politics*, 5 (3): 383–405.

Seymour-Ure, C. (1995) 'Characters and Assassinations: Portrayals of John Major and Neil Kinnock in *The Daily Mirror* and *The Sun*', in I. Crewe and B. Gosschalk (eds), *Political Communications: The General Election Campaign of 1992*, Cambridge: Cambridge University Press.

Seymour-Ure, C. (1997) 'Newspapers: Editorial Opinion in the National Press', in P. Norris and N. Gavin (eds), *Britain Votes 1997*, Oxford: Oxford University Press.

Seymour-Ure, C. (1998) 'Leaders and Leading Articles: Characterisation of John Major and Tony Blair in the Editorials of the National Daily Press', in I. Crewe, B. Gosschalk and J. Bartle (eds), *Political Communications: Why Labour Won the General Election of 1997*, London: Frank Cass.

Shively, W.P. (1998) *The Craft of Political Research*, 4th edn, Englewood Cliffs, NJ: Prentice-Hall.

Slater, D. (1998) 'Analysing Cultural Objects: Content Analysis and Semiotics', in C. Seale (ed.), *Researching Society and Culture*, London: Sage.

Slattery, M. (1986) *Official Statistics*, London: Tavistock Publications.

Smith, D. and Barot, T. (2000) 'A Great Day for Lassie, Ali and Albert Einstein', *The Sunday Times*, 2 January.

Smith, T.M.F. (1996) 'Public Opinion Polls: the UK General Election, 1992', *Journal of the Royal Statistical Society*, 159 (3): 535–545.

Southall, H. (1999) 'Working with Historical Statistics on Poverty and Economic Distress', in D. Dorling and S. Simpson (eds), *Statistics in Society: The Arithmetic of Politics*, London: Arnold.

Stedward, G. (1997) 'On the Record: an Introduction to Interviewing', in P. Burnham (ed.), *Surviving the Research Process in Politics*, London: Pinter.

Stoker, G. (1995) 'Introduction', in D. Marsh and G. Stoker (eds), *Theory and Methods in Political Science*, London: Macmillan.

Swetnam, D. (1995) *How to Write Your Dissertation*, Plymouth: How To Books.

Tant, A.P. (1995) 'The Politics of Official Statistics', *Government and Opposition*, 30 (2): 254–266.

Taylor, B. and Thomson, K. (1999) 'Technical Appendix', in G. Evans and P. Norris (eds), *Critical Elections: British Parties and Voters in Long-term Perspective*, London: Sage.

Thomas, R. (1999) 'The Politics and Reform of Unemployment and Employment Statistics', in D. Dorling and S. Simpson (eds) *Statistics in Society: The Arithmetic of Politics*, London: Arnold.

Townsend, P. (1996) 'The Struggle for Independent Statistics on Poverty', in R. Levitas and W. Guy (eds), *Interpreting Official Statistics*, London: Routledge.

Vickers, R. (1995) 'Using Archives in Political Research', in P. Burnham (ed.), *Surviving the Research Process in Politics*, London: Pinter.

Waller, R. and Criddle, B. (1999) *The Almanac of British Politics*, 6th edn, London: Routledge.

Walsh, D. (1998) 'Doing Ethnography', in C. Seale (ed.), *Researching Society and Culture*, London: Sage.

Ward, S. and Gibson, R. (1998) 'The First Internet Election? UK Political Parties and Campaigning in Cyberspace', in I. Crewe, B. Gosschalk and J. Bartle (eds), *Political Communications: Why Labour Won the General Election of 1997*, London: Frank Cass.

Whiteley, P. and Seyd, P. (1998) 'Labour's Grassroots Campaign in 1997', in D. Denver, J. Fisher, P. Cowley and C. Pattie (eds), *The British Elections and Parties Review*, Volume 8: *The 1997 General Election*, London: Frank Cass.

Widdowfield, R. (1999) 'The Limitations of Official Homelessness Statistics', in D. Dorling and S. Simpson (eds), *Statistics in Society: The Arithmetic of Politics*, London: Arnold.

Wilson, M. (1996) 'Asking Questions', in R. Sapsford and V. Jupp (eds), *Data Collection and Analysis*, London: Sage.

Wring, D. (1997) 'The Media and the Election', in A. Geddes and J. Tonge (eds), *Labour's Landslide*, Manchester: Manchester University Press.

Wring, D., Henn, M. and Weinstein, M. (1999) 'Young People and Contemporary Politics: Committed Scepticism or Engaged Cynicism?', in J. Fisher, P. Cowley, D. Denver and A. Russell (eds), *The British Elections and Parties Review*, Volume 9, London: Frank Cass.

Index